Autism Intervention Every Day!

Autism Intervention Every Day!
Embedding Activities in Daily Routines for Young Children and Their Families

by

Merle J. Crawford, M.S., OTR/L, BCBA, CIMI

and

Barbara Weber, M.S., CCC-SLP, BCBA

·P A U L ·H·
BROOKES
PUBLISHING C°®

Baltimore • London • Sydney

Paul H. Brookes Publishing Co.
Post Office Box 10624
Baltimore, Maryland 21285-0624

www.brookespublishing.com

Typeset by Progressive Publishing Services, Emigsville, Pennsylvania.
Manufactured in the United States of America by
Sheridan Books, Inc., Chelsea, Michigan

Cover images are ©istockphoto/Nadezhda1906/nd3000/Tomwang112/monkeybusinessimages. Other photos are used by permission of the individuals pictured and/or their families.

Clip art © 2016 Jupiterimages Corporation.

The individuals described in this book are composites or real people whose situations are masked and are based on the authors' experiences. In all instances, names and identifying details have been changed to protect confidentiality.

Library of Congress Cataloging-in-Publication Data

The Library of Congress has cataloged the printed edition as follows:

Names: Crawford, Merle J., author. | Weber, Barbara, 1956-
Title: Autism intervention every day! : embedding activities in daily routines for young children and their
     families / by Merle J. Crawford, M.S., OTR/L, BCBA, CIMI and Barbara Weber, M.S., CCC-SLP, BCBA.
Description: Baltimore, Maryland : Paul H. Brookes Publishing Co., 2016. | Includes bibliographical references
     and index.
Identifiers: LCCN 2015049390 (print) | LCCN 2016010897 (ebook) | ISBN 9781598579284 (paperback) |
     ISBN 978-1-68125-190-5 (pdf) | ISBN 978-1-68125-189-9 (epub)
Subjects: LCSH: Children with autism spectrum disorders—Life skills guides. | Children with autism
     spectrum disorders—Family relationships. | Interpersonal relations—Juvenile literature. | BISAC: FAMILY &
     RELATIONSHIPS / Life Stages / Infants & Toddlers. | FAMILY & RELATIONSHIPS / Children with
     Special Needs.
Classification: LCC RJ506.A9 C73 2016 (print) | LCC RJ506.A9 (ebook) | DDC 616.85/88200835—dc23
LC record available at http://lccn.loc.gov/2015049390

British Library Cataloguing in Publication data are available from the British Library.

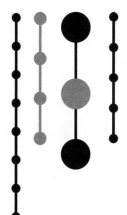

Contents

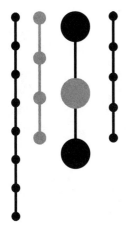

About the
Downloadable Material

Purchasers of this book may download, print, and/or photocopy the blank form in Figure 3.1 for professional use. This material is included with the print book and is also available for print and e-book buyers at **www.brookespublishing.com/crawford/materials**.

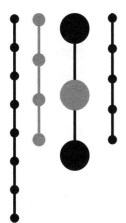

About the Authors

Merle J. Crawford, M.S., OTR/L, BCBA, CIMI, is an occupational therapist who has a private practice in central Pennsylvania. She has a bachelor of science degree in special education and elementary education and a master's degree in occupational therapy. In addition, Ms. Crawford has graduate certificates in applied behavior analysis and autism. She has extensive training in relationship-based interventions and is a Board Certified Behavior Analyst and a Certified Infant Massage Instructor. Ms. Crawford works primarily with infants and toddlers in early intervention, integrating strategies from her varied training when coaching families and working with young children.

Barbara Weber, M.S., CCC-SLP, BCBA, is a speech-language pathologist who has a private practice in central Pennsylvania. She received her bachelor of science degree and master's degree in communication disorders. Ms. Weber has a graduate certificate in applied behavior analysis. She holds the Certificate of Clinical Competence from the American Speech-Language-Hearing Association and is a Board Certified Behavior Analyst. She has worked with children and adults with a variety of disabilities for more than 30 years in school, clinic, and home settings. Ms. Weber works with infants and toddlers as her primary clinical focus and concentrates on collaborative processes to help families integrate routines-based intervention.

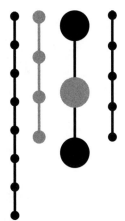

Acknowledgments

MERLE CRAWFORD

Thank you so much to the many children and their families who have taken me on this journey that began with a lack of knowledge about and understanding of autism, which made me feel helpless and uncomfortable and led me to where I am now: intrigued, fascinated, and wanting to know all I can. Thank you to Barb Weber, who shares this fascination and desire to know as much as possible about autism spectrum disorder, for all of her brainstorming, patience, ideas, and hard work that made this book possible. Thanks to Kim Beard, Rachel Bechtel, Donna LeFevre, and G. David Smith for their help and valuable feedback regarding the model of the core deficits of autism presented in this book, as well as the many parents who completed our survey and talked with us about important messages to share. Thank you to Paul H. Brookes Publishing Co. for the enthusiasm and support. Thanks to Christopher, Alyssa, Jeri, Len, Lynn, Chess, and Burnett for all of their support and love. Last, but certainly not least, there is no way to express my immeasurable love and gratitude to my husband, Greg, for all of his love, support, patience, and understanding (as well as the hours and hours of consulting and editing)!

BARBARA WEBER

This book would have not have been possible without all the people who have supported and taught me so much. I want to express my profound gratitude to my husband, Howard, for his endless love and support. Thank you also to Andrea, David, Erin, Nicolas, Rachel, Nick, Sarah, and Michelle for their love and inspiration in all my endeavors. I wish to express my deep appreciation to G. David Smith, Donna LeFevre, Rachel Bechtel, and Kim Beard for providing invaluable insight in reviewing our core deficits model. Thanks so much to Stephanie and Jackson for their special help. Thank you to Pam for sharing her stories with me that have given me a perspective that I could never have had without her. I am deeply grateful to Paul H. Brookes Publishing Co. for the opportunity to work with its expert team once again. Words are not enough to thank Greg Crawford for countless hours of editing, advising, and revising. It is with the deepest gratitude that I thank Merle Crawford for her friendship, dedication, guidance, and brilliance. It is an honor to be her colleague, friend, and coauthor. I am forever grateful to the children and families I work with who have taught me so much. It was my wish that this book reflect their voices and lives, and I sincerely hope I have succeeded.

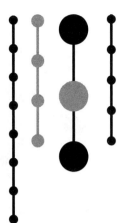

Introduction

This book was written to assist early intervention providers working with young children who are on the autism spectrum or who have characteristics of an autism spectrum disorder (ASD). The purpose of the book is to provide early intervention providers with strategies and tools they can use to coach parents and other caregivers to facilitate the development of critical skills and to manage challenging behaviors. The critical skills in this book differ from those in the authors' earlier book, *Early Intervention Every Day! Embedding Activities in Daily Routines for Young Children and Their Families* (Crawford & Weber, 2014). That book highlighted pivotal skills across six developmental domains from birth through 36 months. This book features skills that are particularly relevant and challenging for young children with autism. These skills provide the foundation for learning to interact, to communicate, and to participate in routines in the home, in preschool, as well as in other community settings. Just as the skills featured in *Early Intervention Every Day!,* the skills in this book can be facilitated throughout typical child and family routines and activities.

There are many books written about autism, and some of these focus on young children. This book is unique in that it incorporates research, coaching, a variety of evidence-based strategies, and a problem-solving approach with vignettes from the authors' many years of experience to help providers and, ultimately, parents and their children. In addition, there are recommendations from parents who have children with autism as well from adults who have autism regarding their perspectives about important issues all early intervention providers should know. The authors have found that success when working with young children who have signs of ASD requires constant assessment, within sessions and over time, of the child's motivation, regulation, and developmental strengths and needs because skill acquisition often does not follow the typical trajectory (e.g., identifying numbers and letters, shapes, or colors before identifying common objects; using words to comment but not to request). This book may be used independently or as a supplement to *Early Intervention Every Day!* and gives the reader information pertaining to autism spectrum and related disorders to help providers analyze a child's abilities and challenges and target core deficits so the child's developmental milestones can be met through participation in daily routines.

The book contains nine chapters. Chapter 1 provides general information about autism spectrum disorder and how young children are diagnosed. "Red flags" and core deficits seen in infants, toddlers, and preschoolers are highlighted. The next chapter provides early interventionists with information so they can support families from suspected diagnosis to connecting with services. Chapter 3 contains information regarding why children with ASD need specific teaching strategies and provides a description of those strategies, many of which are from applied behavior analysis. Key concepts and teaching strategies—including motivation, task analysis, shaping, prompting, reinforcement, behavioral momentum, and the function of behavior—are discussed. Chapter 4 of the book presents a framework and an explanation about the relationships among Regulation; Making Sense of Self, Others, and the Environment; Flexibility; and Social Communication. This theme continues in Chapters 5–8, which contain a format similar to the one presented in *Early Intervention Every Day!* Within those chapters, critical skills are presented along with research findings, information about the relevance to young children with autism, and practical suggestions for providers to coach parents and other caregivers regarding ways to practice the skills during daily routines, including bath time, bedtime, book time, community outings, dressing and diapering, grooming and hygiene, household activities, mealtime/snack time, and playtime. Ideas for monitoring progress are also presented. In the last chapter, the problem-solving approach is further discussed so providers can help families with common challenges that occur during daily routines and activities, including birthday parties, community outings, and travel. The topics chosen are from the authors' many years of experience derived from conversations with families and include strategies related to stereotypies and other behaviors that families often report as challenging.

In the introduction of *Early Intervention Every Day!,* the authors stated that they "hope readers will find this book so useful it resides, ready to provide ideas, dog-eared in the early intervention provider's car" (Crawford & Weber, 2014, p. x). The authors share that hope in regard to this book. They hope this book will support providers, families, and others who work with or care for young children who have a diagnosis of autism or for those children who have similarly challenging behavioral and/or learning characteristics that necessitate critical analysis of behavior and specific teaching strategies to help the children reach their potential.

REFERENCE

Crawford, M.J., & Weber, B. (2014). *Early intervention every day! Embedding activities in daily routines for young children and their families.* Baltimore, MD: Paul H. Brookes Publishing Co.

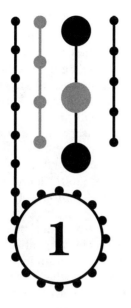

Autism and Early Intervention

1

Early intervention (EI) providers bring unique expertise and experience to the children and families with whom they work. Knowledge about and experience in working with young children who are on the autism spectrum vary. Some providers feel quite comfortable working with children on the autism spectrum, whereas others do not believe they have the needed skills. Those who believe they do not have the needed skills may pass up referrals for children diagnosed with autism and instead prefer to work with children with challenges for which they have expertise: perhaps children with feeding challenges, medical issues, physical challenges, or sensory impairments. However, in some instances, an EI provider may work with a child who initially does not show "red flags" for being on the autism spectrum, and, as time elapses, the provider may find him- or herself challenged to provide strategies to achieve outcomes. For example, a physical therapist may have successfully helped a family facilitate skills such as sitting, crawling, and walking, but when coaching the family to help the child with higher level skills that require following directions and imitation, the provider and parents may find themselves struggling to facilitate the child's motor development. Thus, it is important that all providers have an understanding of autism and related disorders and recommended practices regarding autism in EI.

According to Daniels and Mandell (2014), in their reviews of 42 studies from 1990 to 2012, the mean age of diagnosis for autism spectrum disorder (ASD) ranged from 38 to 120 months. They cited a trend toward earlier diagnosis and discussed a variety of reasons why children are not diagnosed earlier. In the authors' (Crawford's and Weber's) experiences working in EI, how parents proceed after providers discuss the red flags of autism varies. Some families want to get or rule out a diagnosis for their child as soon as they suspect autism or soon after an EI provider discusses concerns regarding an ASD. Other parents are hesitant, as they think they are receiving the needed services for their children regardless of a diagnosis or they do not want their children to receive a label at such a young age. Though it is the parents' choice regarding how to proceed once they are aware of the concerns, all EI providers must have an understanding of ASD and young children in order to provide support and resources.

In the *Diagnostic and Statistical Manual of Mental Disorders, Fifth Edition* (*DSM-5;* American Psychiatric Association [APA], 2013), diagnostic criteria for ASD include "persistent deficits in social communication and social interaction" and "restricted, repetitive patterns of behavior, interests, or activities," with symptoms presenting in "the early developmental period" (p. 50). These deficits cause "clinically significant impairment in social, occupational, or other important areas of current functioning" (APA, p. 50) that are not explained solely by an intellectual disability or global developmental delay. The *DSM-5* cites examples of behaviors that are applicable to infants and toddlers, including abnormalities in eye contact, lining up toys, flipping objects, echolalia, extreme distress at small changes, difficulties with transitions, preoccupation with unusual objects, and hyper- or hyporeactivity to sensory input or unusual interests in sensory aspects of the environment.

Many studies have looked at red flags in order to identify infants and toddlers who have ASD. For example, Wetherby, Watt, Morgan, and Shumway (2007) found that by 18–24 months, there are five social communication core deficits in children with autism: "gaze shift, gaze point/follow, rate of communicating, acts for joint attention, and inventory of gestures" (p. 973). Trillingsgaard, Sørensen, Němec, and Jørgensen (2005) found red flags for ASD if a child does not exhibit the following indicators by 24 months "during a professional semi-structured play interaction": "smiles in response to a smile; responds to his/her name; follows pointing; looks to 'read' faces for information when cheated; initiates requesting non-verbal behavior; joins functional play with miniature toys with an adult; initiates requesting verbal and non-verbal behaviours" (p. 71).

Autism Speaks, an advocacy organization whose web site contains a great deal of information for parents and professionals, presented a list of red flags, including the following (2015b):

> No big smiles or other warm, joyful expressions by six months or thereafter
>
> No back-and-forth sharing of sounds, smiles, or other facial expressions by nine months
>
> No babbling by 12 months
>
> No back-and-forth gestures such as pointing, showing, reaching, or waving by 12 months
>
> No words by 16 months
>
> No meaningful two-word phrases (not including imitating or repeating) by 24 months
>
> Any loss of speech, babbling, or social skills at any age

The Centers for Disease Control and Prevention (CDC; 2014) delineates other red flags, advising that people with autism might exhibit the following behaviors at an early age:

> Not respond to their name by 12 months of age
>
> Not point at objects to show interest (point at an airplane flying over) by 14 months
>
> Not play "pretend" games (pretend to "feed" a doll) by 18 months
>
> Avoid eye contact and want to be alone
>
> Have trouble understanding other people's feelings or talking about their own feelings
>
> Have delayed speech and language skills
>
> Repeat words or phrases over and over (echolalia)
>
> Give unrelated answers to questions
>
> Get upset by minor changes
>
> Have obsessive interests
>
> Flap their hands, rock their body, or spin in circles
>
> Have unusual reactions to the way things sound, smell, taste, look, or feel

In 2007, Johnson and Myers published a comprehensive article in *Pediatrics* to educate physicians about autism, providing "background information, including definition, history, epidemiology, diagnostic criteria, early signs, neuropathologic aspects, and etiologic possibilities in autism spectrum disorder," an "algorithm to help the pediatrician develop a strategy for early identification of children with autism spectrum disorder," and a clinical report that addressed management of children with ASD (p. 1183). Since its publication, routine screening has become common at well-child visits and often results in a referral for further evaluation and/or referral for EI. The type of evaluation a child receives often varies depending upon where a child lives and resources in the area. Two widely used screening tools are the Modified Checklist for Autism in Toddlers–Revised (M-CHAT-R; Robins, Fein, Barton, & Green, 2001) and the Brief Infant-Toddler Social and Emotional Assessment (BITSEA; Briggs-Gowan, Carter, Irwin, Wachtel, & Cicchetti, 2004). The M-CHAT-R, designed for toddlers between 16 and 30 months, is a set of 20 yes/no questions asked of the child's parent and administered by a physician or other professional. The M-CHAT-R's follow-up questionnaire (M-CHAT-R/F; Robins, Fein, & Barton, 2009) is administered when the child fails any item. The BITSEA, designed for children ages 12 months to 35 months and 30 days, reveals both social-emotional problems and competencies. For children who need further assessment, the administration of the Autism Diagnostic Interview–Revised (ADI-R; Rutter, Le Couteur, & Lord, 2003) and the Autism Diagnostic Observation Scale, Second Edition (ADOS-2; Lord et al., 2012) has been considered the "gold standard" for diagnosing ASD (Falkmer, Anderson, Falkmer, & Horlin, 2013). The ADI-R is a semistructured caregiver interview consisting of 93 questions and is appropriate for use with children who exhibit cognitive skills of at least approximately 18 months, and the ADOS-2 is a semistructured assessment administered to individuals 12 months and older.

Some children who exhibit red flags will receive an autism diagnosis, but others will not. In the authors' experiences, many children exhibit some of the characteristics of ASD but not enough to fit the diagnostic criteria during the infant to toddler years. Some young children receive a diagnosis of a global developmental delay and then later receive an autism diagnosis—sometimes by the same diagnostician and sometimes by another. Guthrie, Swineford, Nottke, and Wetherby (2013) discussed reasons a diagnosis may change over time, including the experience of the clinician, whether a standardized test is utilized, changes in severity of symptoms over time, and whether the evaluation occurred in multiple settings, such as in the home and in a clinic. Another consideration regarding diagnoses is that, to date, there is little research regarding the very early signs and symptoms of other disorders that manifest in atypical behavior. For example, bipolar disorder and obsessive compulsive disorder are not typically diagnosed until a child is older, yet many times parents report atypical behaviors occurring when their children were infants and toddlers (Faedda, Baldessarini, Glovinsky, & Austin, 2004; Mian, Godoy, Briggs-Gowan, & Carter, 2011).

The causes of autism continue to be investigated by many researchers who are focusing on genetic and environmental risk factors. Epidemiologic studies have provided important information that warrants further investigation. For example, advanced age of the parents has been found to be a risk factor for ASD, and further study is needed to determine if this is due to a specific genetic mutation and/or because some individuals who marry later in life have mild traits of being on the autism spectrum (Sucksmith, Roth, & Hoekstra, 2011).

Discovering different phenotypes for ASD is another focus for researchers. Variability exists in the severity of deficits in language, cognition, social skills, and repetitive behaviors. Researchers are also examining regression of skills in autism. Kern, Geier, and Geier (2014) found in their literature review that the reported percentage of children with autism who exhibited regression during the second year ranged widely from 15% to 62%. Though research is needed to discover more about autism, the heterogeneity of the diagnosis is conveyed by the popular saying, "When you've met one person with autism, you've met one person with autism."

This individuality in ASD is a very important tenet for all early interventionists. In the authors' experience, many times a specific tool or strategy known to be effective with some children with autism is used without looking at the individual child's strengths and needs. An example of this was seen when a child started at a new preschool program. On the first day, the teacher used sign language and a picture schedule, both of which were unfamiliar to him, rather than asking his mother what makes transitions easier. Her answer would have been to tell him what is coming next by using language such as "first bathroom, then more bike" and giving him a day or two to understand the routine rather than introducing him to a system he did not understand or need.

Not only does an EI provider need to be well versed in understanding autism spectrum and related disorders, he or she also needs to know how to implement services according to recommended practices. When one researches the topic of teaching strategies and autism, one finds two types of intervention. The first type is comprehensive treatment models such as the Early Start Denver Model (ESDM; Rogers & Dawson, 2010), the Learning Experiences and Alternative Program for Preschoolers and their Parents (LEAP; Hoyson, Jamieson, & Strain, 1984), and the Treatment and Education of Autistic and Communication Handicapped Children (TEACCH) Program (Mesibov, Shea, & Schopler, 2005), which are "conceptually organized packages of practices and components designed to address a broad array of skills and abilities" (Odom, Boyd, Hall, & Hume, 2010, p. 425). The other type is focused intervention practices, which are "designed to produce specific behavioral or developmental outcomes" (Odom, Collet-Klingenberg, Rogers, & Hatton, 2010, p. 276). Examples include techniques such as video modeling, prompting, reinforcement, and visual supports.

Recommended practice dictates that intervention be evidence based, and both the American Academy of Pediatrics (Myers & Johnson, 2007) and the National Research Council Committee on Educational Interventions for Children with Autism (2001) have published research regarding which methods from both categories are considered evidence based. These publications are quite useful for professionals and for families; however, as Strain, Schwartz, and Barton (2011) pointed out, the publications do not ensure that children with ASD

> Have access to systematic and effective instruction. Systematic and effective instruction does not just mean that educators have toolboxes full of the strategies that have been identified as being evidence based by a national panel. It requires that educators know how to identify the instructional needs of their students, develop instructional plans to address those needs, and then match the needs of their students with the instructional strategies that they have at their disposal. (p. 324)

Some treatment models and intervention practices are considered behavior based, whereas others are considered developmental. Some bridge a gap that has historically been controversial and combine both approaches. As stated by Leach (2012), "There is much to be learned from the work of leading researchers and practitioners from both the behavioral and developmental perspectives, and the strengths from both perspectives can contribute to quality interventions for young children with ASD" (p. 70). As Leach points out—and as is confirmed in the experience of this book's authors (Crawford and Weber), who have had extensive training in both behavioral and developmental approaches—many strategies are used in both approaches, though the terminology may be different.

Some of the treatment models and interventions in the literature have been deemed evidenced based with older children; however, some have had little or no research regarding use with infants and/or toddlers. If one compares cognitive and communication processes, learning characteristics, and daily routines, significant differences exist between infants and toddlers and preschoolers (Zwaigenbaum et al., 2009). Thus, EI providers must synthesize their knowledge about development, autism research, and recommended practices. One of the recommended practices in EI is coaching. According to Rogers and Vismara (2014),

> The birth-to-3 world of public intervention services is currently working from a client-centered, adult-learning framework rather than an expertise driven framework, reflecting the family-centered values explicit in IDEA. As articulated by Rush and Shelden (2011), whose work is well known and quite popular in the birth-to-3 world, coaching has replaced parent training as the preferred framework for parent-professional interactions, vis-à-vis supporting young children with disabilities. (p. 759)

Rogers and Vismara go on to ask,

> How do we integrate parent-centric values of coaching and individualization for varying adult learning styles with the emphasis on empirically based practices, consistency, and adult behavior change that lie at the heart of the ASD parent intervention approaches? This is an active point of dialogue and practice revision in many early ASD intervention groups, and we look forward to the syntheses that will begin to emerge in the literature in the next few years. (p. 760)

The authors (Crawford and Weber) have found coaching strategies to be very effective with many families. The caregiver's needs, family needs and resources, and caregiver interactions within intervention approaches influence efficacy of EI (Strauss et al., 2012). Legislation and policy have underlined the need for collaborative relationships with caregivers (Individuals with Disabilities Education Improvement Act [IDEA] of 2004, PL 108–446). It is now a widely accepted practice in EI to build the provider's understanding of adult learning so that he or she can help the caregiver learn how to help the child through his or her input within daily routines. Coaching entails using adult learning strategies to promote the caregiver's ability to reflect upon his or her actions for effective change and to create a plan for further development by joint planning with the provider, observation of the child, planning actions he or she will practice, reflecting on the successes or lack of success, and feedback between the caregiver and the provider (Rush & Shelden, 2011). The coaching service delivery model focuses on strengthening caregiver–child exchanges. This caregiver-focused model requires the provider to know evidence-based interventions that help support child development and to be skilled in using the coaching process in collaboration with the important caregivers (Woods, Wilcox, Friedman, & Murch, 2011).

There are two components of coaching: It is family centered and it uses family identified contexts. Family-centered practice entails asking for and respecting caregivers' views, ensuring equal participation by the caregivers in the decision-making process, and recognizing caregivers' rights to make decisions (Dunst, Trivette, & Hamby, 2007). Family-identified contexts include using community and daily routines to facilitate growth and development (e.g., a provider may help a family embed following directions into bath time or gross motor development into an outing to the park). *Natural environments* is the term used in IDEA 2004 Part C to refer to settings that are typical for all infants and toddlers. Children learn through participating in their everyday activities, which provides children with multiple opportunities for intervention throughout each day (Woods, 2008).

In working with children with ASD, the authors have found that many everyday occurrences are affected by the child's skills and preferences (e.g., resisting wearing warmer pajamas when the season changes, being a selective eater, reacting to noise at a birthday party, having difficulties with transitions). Coaching caregivers within these routines provides the learning and support needed to facilitate changes within everyday experiences. One of the authors worked with a family who had several EI providers in the home in addition to providers from the behavioral health system who worked on discrete skills while the child sat at the table. When the author asked the parents about the challenges they had, they cited experiences with challenging behaviors during frequently occurring routines such as getting out of the tub at bath time, going on shopping trips, and wearing new shoes. The parents reported that no one was helping them with these challenges, so the therapist scheduled her sessions during bath time, shopping, and at times new shoes would be worn. The therapist and parents collaborated to find solutions that worked for the family. The parents were grateful and appreciative of the support, which made their lives easier and fostered a positive relationship with their child.

Coaching within daily routines is an efficient process for quickly solving problems and enables caregivers to learn strategies to help their children develop new skills in natural learning contexts. EI providers often need to make families aware that EI services can and should occur within family routines. In the authors' experiences, some families embrace this easily, whereas with others, it is a process. The families may have experience with other models of services, such as going to an outpatient clinic, or they may have had EI providers who do not have experience using coaching and a family-centered model. It is helpful when the philosophy of EI is explained and reiterated to families from the first point of contact, through the individualized family service plan (IFSP) process, and during sessions, via asking questions about the child's everyday experiences.

It can be challenging to integrate family routines into therapy time due to schedule constraints. The authors have found that developing a plan with the caregivers for the next session has helped facilitate coaching within routines. For example, the authors have asked caregivers if they can plan for the child to brush his or her teeth, get dressed, have breakfast, sweep the floors, or go grocery shopping with the caregivers during an upcoming session. Families' belief systems can also affect routines-based intervention. One of the authors worked with a mother who thought that therapy should be doing tasks like puzzles and working on drills such as imitation and pointing to request crackers. She thought that other activities were "a waste of time," as her son was not learning enough. She was very reluctant to implement strategies and skills into daily routines, but after persistent encouragement, the mother agreed to dress her son after the therapist arrived. The therapist immediately noticed that the mother was in a hurry to get the child dressed, the child was not attending to the process, and there was no interaction between mother and child. The therapist suggested that the mother turn the child toward her, which then resulted in intermittent attention to the mother's face. The mother was then coached to take the time to label clothing and body parts and to embed simple directions such as "give me your arm" and "hands up." The therapist suggested that the mother use the sign for "all done" when finished dressing the child, which the child previously had used only when songs ended with his music therapist. The mother later remarked, "I cannot believe what a difference those small changes made. It's as if he is 'there,' not somewhere else in his own little world." She also told the therapist that during an upcoming vacation she planned to "do that dressing thing. Like turn him toward me and make sure he is 'there.' We can do that when we take a walk, or get ice cream or with anything."

Many parents embrace the coaching model and are very successful at integrating strategies to facilitate their child's development throughout a variety of daily routines. Some parents seek resources to obtain a certain number of hours a week, often based on the National Research Council's (2001) report that recommended at least 25 hours per week of "active engagement in intensive instructional programming" (p. 219). This recommendation has been a topic for many researchers, administrators, developmental pediatricians, and other professionals in the field, as interpretation of what constitutes "active engagement" varies widely and the type of intervention that is appropriate for infants and toddlers is quite different from the intervention needed for older children. According to Leach (2012), many professionals and caregivers erroneously interpret the recommended 25 hours per week to mean one-to-one instruction. Many people do not realize that active engagement can occur with parents and other caregivers during embedded learning opportunities at home and in the community and are unaware of the role that EI providers can play in coaching families to successfully engage their children in everyday learning opportunities. As Strain et al. (2012) suggested,

> The challenge to the research community, however, is to not attempt to answer the question of intensity for toddlers with ASD and their families with a prescription of hours but rather, with a process for judging support needs and whether those needs are addressed. (p. 326)

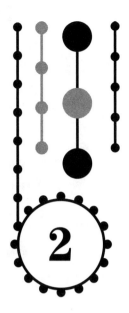

Supporting Parents from Suspicions to Diagnosis to Services

Often, before an ASD diagnosis is given, the provider, the family, or both may be questioning the child's behavior and/or development. Concerns may include communication delays, repetitive behaviors, and/or a lack of interest in social interaction. Consistently asking caregivers about their concerns, priorities, and challenges will likely yield the forum to discuss developmental issues. After concerns arise, the next step usually is to determine whether the signs and symptoms warrant further evaluation to rule out diagnosis of ASD. This process is uncomfortable for many EI providers to initiate, and a study by Tomlin, Koch, Raches, Minshawi, and Swiezy (2013) found that EI providers felt unprepared to do so.

EI providers are not qualified to provide a diagnosis but often must disclose to families, at an evaluation or when providing ongoing services, that a child has red flags. In some instances, parents are relieved when EI providers begin the conversation, and other times, parents do not welcome the discussion. When serving on an initial evaluation team, one of the authors found it helpful to ask whether anyone had brought up concerns to the family about the child's repetitive play, tantrums, difficulties with eye contact, or whatever red flags the child exhibited. Many times, this evoked a comment such as "Yes, my mother thinks he has autism." It was also helpful to ask if any other family members had showed similar delays in communication. Sometimes, a parent would respond by saying that a cousin or other relative was similar and then would go on to say that person had a diagnosis of autism. When the parent brought up the term *autism,* it was less stressful for the provider than when the provider needed to introduce the term. In the latter instance, the parent was more likely to be surprised, shocked, or unprepared for the discussion.

Many times, parents will ask providers if they think the child has autism. Providers must tell parents that they are not able to make a diagnosis, but they should be honest about concerns they have regarding red flags. Even when providers state that they are unable to diagnose, parents look to them for opinions based on their experiences. A mother of a child who was diagnosed at age 2 had recently started attending a preschool program when she expressed her frustration to one of the authors. She said she had asked her daughter's team if they thought her daughter had autism and no one would answer her question; instead, team members asked her if she wanted further evaluation. This mother was in the process of learning about autism and wanted to know the team's opinion about her daughter's strengths and needs related to the diagnosis. She thought the team was concerned about saying "the right thing" rather than answering her question. To help providers with this difficult conversation, the CDC (n.d.) gives the following advice in its *Tips for Talking with Parents*:

- Highlight some of the child's strengths, letting the parent know what the child does well.

- Use materials like the "Learn the Signs. Act Early." fact sheets. This will help the parent know that you are basing your comments on facts and not just feelings.

- Talk about specific behaviors that you have observed in caring for the child. Use the milestones fact sheets as a guide....

- Try to make it a discussion. Pause a lot, giving the parent time to think and to respond.

- Expect that if the child is the oldest in the family, the parent might not have enough experience to know the milestones the child should be reaching.

- Listen to and watch the parent to decide on how to proceed. Pay attention to tone of voice and body language.

- This might be the first time the parent has become aware that the child might have a delay. Give the parent time to think about this and even speak with the child's other caregivers.

THE EVALUATION PROCESS

Young children may be referred by an EI provider or a primary care physician to a neurologist, developmental pediatrician, or clinical psychologist for an evaluation to determine a diagnosis. Some EI programs have contracts with or may provide a list of contacts for psychologists, developmental pediatricians, or agencies that can provide a diagnosis of ASD. At times, the family may begin the discussion with the pediatrician, though in other situations, the doctor may initiate the concern. Resources vary in communities; according to the Simons Foundation Autism Research Initiative, there is a shortage of evaluators and health care providers who have expertise in autism, and this is creating a "diagnosis bottleneck" (DeWeerdt, 2014). This bottleneck often means that parents have to wait for long periods of time before a diagnosis is confirmed or ruled out. During this time, EI providers can help support families and caregivers by answering their questions and focusing on the parents' priorities and the child's strengths and needs. Though receiving a diagnosis may have an immense impact on families, the diagnosis itself does not change the child's specific needs at a given time. For example, a 2-year-old child who is not yet communicating with gestures or words needs strategies to build communication skills whether the child has autism, an unspecified developmental delay, or Down syndrome. EI providers can help support families through this process as they focus on the child's strengths and needs related to learning rather than on the diagnostic label the child may receive.

EI providers often are able to provide support to families during the process of receiving a diagnosis. Parents have reported a great deal of anxiety before the feedback session after their child's evaluation (Abbot, Bernard, & Forge, 2013), and one study found a subgroup of parents who exhibited moderate to high levels of posttraumatic stress symptoms following a diagnosis (Casey et al., 2012). The time following the diagnosis is when parents have a critical need for information on ASD and support in understanding the information (Bradford, 2010). The Internet is a common source of information for those families who have access, yet the information is not always accurate (Reichow et al., 2012). Families struggle with determining what is high-quality, research-based information and what may be anecdotal in nature. The endorsement of a special diet, vitamins, and other information promising positive outcomes is alluring and convincing, and an estimated 32%–92% of parents of children with ASD try alternative methods (Matson, Adams, Williams, & Rieske, 2013). Caregivers will find many statements on the Internet about specific treatments, although safety and benefits of treatments for ASD and other developmental conditions often are not based upon empirical evidence (Di Pietro, Whiteley, Mizgalewicz, & Illes, 2013). Providers can help families by recommending resources that are supported by empirical evidence and, when parents choose treatments that have unsubstantiated benefits, providers should ask questions and provide information in nonjudgmental ways.

AFTER THE DIAGNOSIS

Families may be inundated with recommendations for the type, duration, and intensity of services and may feel significant stress in attempting to make decisions that are right for them. Many families report feeling that they "must" procure all of the recommended services and yet they are often left to cobble together services from a variety of systems, often without the support to do so. For example, Maya's developmental pediatrician recommended 20 hours of in-home therapy as well as private speech and occupational therapies outside of EI. Her parents, who had two other children and worked full time, struggled to find the time to find service providers who took their insurance and also struggled to find the time to meet Maya's needs and balance the needs of the rest of the family. Information and recommendations from the pediatrician, EI providers, behavioral health personnel, family, and friends may or may not complement each other. Even within the EI system itself, there may be a lack of collaboration and coordination among team members that results in gaps in development and splinter skills.

In addition, providers sometimes focus on the developmental trajectory across developmental domains without providing support for daily behavioral challenges that are having an impact on the family. For example, Cooper's EI providers gave wonderful suggestions for incorporating strategies to facilitate his developmental skills but did not realize that mealtimes and transitions in and out of the tub and car seat were immensely stressful for everyone. His EI providers assumed that Cooper's behavioral needs were being met through the behavioral health system. Countless parents find themselves in a position in which they quickly must not only learn about a variety of systems and professions but must also spend a great deal of time and energy being the case manager to coordinate the various people and systems. A mother told one of the authors, "I hate Mondays now. Mondays mean phone calls, and I have to fight for everything my child needs. I have so much to do, and these phone calls take forever. I can feel myself age through all of this. It really takes a toll."

Making Decisions About Treatment Approaches

There is consensus among researchers that services for young children with autism should focus on social communication, and there are many treatment programs and strategies that do so. These treatment programs and strategies lie along a continuum with the behavioral intervention of discrete trials on one end and developmental approaches on the other (Wetherby & Woods, 2008).

Discrete Trial Training (DTT), also known as discrete trial instruction (DTI), was developed by Lovaas (1987). DTT and DTI teach children to exhibit specific responses in the presence of specific conditions, utilizing prompts and motivation to ensure the response will occur. For example, Lydia was taught to match identical pictures using DTT. Her special instructor began by placing a picture on the table, handing Lydia an identical picture, and saying "match." She physically helped Lydia place her picture on top of the match and then gave Lydia an enthusiastic high-five. Over time, the special instructor systematically decreased her assistance, increased the number of picture choices, and decreased the frequency at which she gave high-fives until Lydia was able to independently match a set of five pictures at a time.

Many people think of DTT as synonymous with applied behavior analysis (ABA). Contrary to popular belief, ABA is not synonymous with one method or technique. ABA-based interventions range from programs that are conducted in a one-to-one treatment setting to more naturalistic programs that include typically developing children as models. Some EI providers are Board Certified Behavior Analysts, and others have experience and training in the principles of behavior analysis. Effective instructional and behavior management strategies often are applications of ABA.

ABA consists of seven dimensions: applied (socially significant in terms of improving lives), behavioral (based on a behavior that needs to be improved and that is measurable), analytic (a change in behavior that is the result of the intervention), technological (described in a way so that it is replicable), conceptually systematic (derived from relevant principles), effective (significantly changes behavior positively), and generality (demonstrated over time and across people and environments (Cooper, Heron, & Heward, 2007; Leach, 2012). An important component of ABA is the three-term contingency: the antecedent, the behavior, and the consequence. This contingency, known as the ABCs of behavior, can be seen in the following example. Rosie's father said good-bye to her when he left for work and Rosie waved, which resulted in her father smiling and blowing her a kiss. The antecedent was Rosie's father saying good-bye, the behavior was Rosie waving, and the consequence was her father's smile and kiss. Changing antecedents and/or consequences results in behavior changes. DTT, one of the types of ABA, breaks skills into discrete tasks that typically are taught using repetition and specific prompts that are faded to ensure success and mastery. Applied verbal behavior incorporates DTT along with a classification of language identified by B.F. Skinner (1957). Four of the types of language Skinner identified are relevant to very young children: mands (requests), tacts (labels), echoics (repeated sounds, words, or phrases), and intraverbals (filling in sounds, words, or phrases or answering questions) (Barbera, 2007; Leach). Pivotal Response Treatment (PRT; Koegel & Koegel, 2012) is a type of ABA that, unlike DTT, occurs during natural routines and emphasizes naturally occurring consequences or reinforcers (Leach, 2012).

Because PRT is implemented during typical routines, it is on the continuum closer to developmental approaches. Wagner, Wallace, and Rogers (2014) identified five common features in many approaches that identified themselves as developmental: they follow the sequence of typical development, they use principles of developmental science, they are relationship based, they are child centered, and they are play based. Developmental approaches include the ESDM (Rogers & Dawson, 2010); Developmental, Individual Differences, Relationship-Based Model (DIRFloortime; Wieder & Greenspan, 2001); Hanen's More Than Words (Carter et al., 2011); Joint Attention Mediated Learning (JAML; Schertz, 2005); Joint Attention Symbolic Play Engagement and Regulation (JASPER; Kasari, Gulsrud, Wong, Kwon, & Locke, 2010); Relationship Development Intervention (RDI; Gutstein & Sheely, 2002); Responsive Education and Prelinguistic Milieu Teaching (RPMT) or milieu teaching (Schreibman & Ingersoll, 2011); Responsive Teaching (RT; Mahoney & MacDonald, 2005); Social Communication, Emotional Regulation, and Transactional Support (SCERTS©; Prizant, Wetherby, Rubin, Laurent, & Rydell, 2006); and TEACCH (Marcus & Schopler, 2007). On the Autism Speaks web site, ESDM is described as a program that "integrates a relationship-focused developmental model with the well-validated practices of Applied Behavior Analysis" (Autism Speaks, 2015a), a testament to the trend to blend approaches.

Many treatment approaches have been studied with older children, but research with infants and toddlers has been sparse (Boyd, Odom, Humphreys, & Sam, 2010). In addition, treatment approaches are often based on comprehensive treatment packages or "brand name" approaches. When families and professionals attempt to implement the intervention approach used in the studies, they often are unable to determine which part of the package is responsible for the changes, are unable to find the exact package, and/or are unable to replicate procedures as done exactly in the study (Rogers & Vismara, 2014).

The frequency and intensity of services for infants and toddlers varies greatly. There is an assumption that more is better; however, there is little empirical support for this assumption (Rogers & Vismara, 2014). In their report, the National Research Council (2001) recommended that a child with ASD should have education services of at least 25 hours a week, 12 months a year, whereby the child is engaged in "systematically planned, developmentally appropriate educational activity aimed toward identified objectives" (p. 220). The council also stated that the location and content "should be determined on an individual basis, depending on characteristics of both the child and the family" (p. 220). This report referred to individualized education programs (IEPs) but not IFSPs, perhaps because an autism diagnosis in children younger than 3 years was uncommon at that time.

In the authors' experience, many diagnosticians, because of the National Research Council's recommendations, make the same recommendations for children with autism without considering that the recommendations were made for children older than 3 years. In addition, recommendations from diagnosticians sometimes do not consider the child's environment. There are parents who are extremely competent in actively engaging children throughout the day and other parents who need more support. Similarly, there are children who are in child care and preschool programs with personnel who are able to meet the needs of children with ASD, whereas there are other programs with staff who do not have the expertise, experience, or support. Thus, the frequency and intensity of services needed for a child must be based on multiple factors, not simply a diagnosis. Recommended practice for infants and toddlers involves coaching families and caregivers in ways to implement intervention throughout daily routines, and research is being conducted to determine the efficacy of parent-implemented intervention within this model. Many infants and toddlers in EI receive services for 3–4 hours per week, during which time parents learn how to embed intervention strategies throughout the day, which provides the means for achieving the recommended 25 hours of active engagement (Wetherby & Woods, 2006). Though parent-implemented programs have not yet shown the impact that more long-term, intensive, therapist-delivered programs have, this does not mean they cannot be as effective because the parent-implemented programs have not been delivered at the same frequency and intensity. In addition, these studies face methodological challenges that affect their findings (Rogers & Vismara, 2014).

Family Stress

Getting a diagnosis, sifting through information regarding autism and autism interventions, and trying to make the best decisions can be quite stressful for parents. During one of the last sessions before their daughter turned 3 and was close to moving from EI to the preschool program, parents asked one of the authors if they should pursue outpatient therapy in addition to what the preschool program would be providing. The EI provider said that she believed this to be a decision they needed to make based on their daughter's needs, their priorities for her, and their schedules. She reminded the parents that they could start with one decision and change their minds. The EI provider asked what they did when their son who also has ASD turned 3. Both parents began to reflect on how, when their son was diagnosed, "they hit the ground running with PT [physical therapy], OT [occupational therapy], speech therapy, a Board Certified Behavior Analyst, a behavior aide, the preschool program, aquatic therapy, and therapeutic horseback riding because they did not want to miss anything and wanted their families and others to know they were doing what they could." The doctor who had diagnosed their son told them that critical development occurred before age 5, and they felt tremendous pressure to take advantage of any service they could. They talked about how during this time there was a enormous amount of stress on the family, their marriage, and their health. They were glad they realized this and downsized their team and their activities before the stress took an even larger toll. They offered the advice that parents should balance the needs of the whole family with the needs of the child or children with autism, saying, "Do what you feel is right for you. You need to find a balance. Don't let what others think cloud what is right for you. It can drive you crazy. Don't use all your energy for things that you can't change."

Another parent, who was flooded with unfamiliar acronyms during the process of her child's evaluation, asked how she could get her child "an ABA." She had received recommendations and needed support to help her understand the terminology and the resources as she tried to make sense of the services and those who provide the services. Similarly, another parent who was told her child should have ABA frequently asked during sessions, "Was that ABA, what you just did?" She wondered if she was getting ABA through EI services, and struggled to identify what she should be receiving, what ABA looked like, and whether her child was receiving the services she wanted him to have. Another family thought that tasks such as pointing to pictures in books, matching shapes, and doing puzzles was equivalent to ABA. This family was resistant to embedding strategies into daily routines, thinking that time would be wasted not doing ABA if the child was not involved in doing puzzles and similar activities.

Another stressor, in addition to the confusion of being inundated by the "alphabet soup" of ASD treatment that is related to service delivery, is the potential change in the dynamics of the family relationships. This can occur with partners or with members of the extended family. The authors have noticed that, at times, when the primary caregiver who participates in EI sessions assumes the role of "instructor" to the other caregiver, the partner may show feelings of resentment, anger, and/or inadequacy regarding being told what to do or how to parent. The authors have overheard comments such as "Not like that," "Don't do that," or "You have to...." In addition, different parenting styles or roles may be another source of conflict. As one mother said, "Since John works so much, he thinks it's playtime when he is home with Evelyn. I am the one who has to do the hard work during the day, and he has no idea what I go through. She does not even tantrum for him like she does with me. Why should she? It's all fun and games with Daddy." Another mother shared, "Even though I tell Grandma she should be telling him to say the word when he wants juice, she just gets it for him. She does not think he should have to talk to get what he wants." Social work services or counseling may be needed to help resolve such conflicts.

According to Bailey (2008), in addition to the stressors related to service delivery, parents who have young children with ASD frequently report concerns regarding finances, gaining access to appropriate health care, time management, and balancing employment with the impact of the child's needs, which may require taking time off from work for appointments, decreasing work hours, or, in some cases, leaving a job permanently to care for the child. Some parents, after a diagnosis is made, feel angry about the loss of time for intervention prior to the diagnosis. Some families feel relief that their concerns have been validated, whereas others are surprised or disappointed. Guilt is also a feeling that has been reported by parents of children with autism, and this feeling may be a barrier to participation in the EI process (Durand, 2014).

Some parents, after getting reports from preschool or child care programs that their children are struggling, worry that the perception is that they are at fault. They then become disengaged, thinking that the child care or preschool staff feel they are "bad parents." The parents of a child who had challenging behavior in his child care setting were distraught after their son's teachers sent home their daily notes highlighting all of his challenging behaviors. During a session at the child care center, the teacher made positive comments about the improvement in the child's behavior. The EI provider suggested the teacher write her comment on the daily note, and the teacher stated the notes were only for problem behaviors. The EI provider told the teacher how upset the parents were about the daily bad news, and the teacher said she would make a point to tell them positive comments when they arrived at the end of the day.

Some families may have more than one child with special needs and, in some cases, more than one child with autism. Ozonoff et al. (2011) found, in a study of 664 infants, that 18.7% of those who had at least one older sibling with ASD also received an autism diagnosis. They found being a male and having more than one older sibling with ASD to be the strongest predictors for a child to receive an ASD diagnosis. The added concerns of a sibling's risk for developing ASD and/or caring for multiple children with special needs are significant stressors for families.

In addition to concerns about their other children's risk for autism, some parents have concerns about how a child's autism affects his or her siblings. In a review of the literature, Tsao, Davenport, and Schmiege (2012) found both negative and positive impacts of having a sibling with autism. Negative impacts include embarrassment regarding the behavior of the child with autism, less interaction between siblings, and increased loneliness noted by the sibling without autism, whereas positive impacts include healthy self-concepts, less competitiveness, and good academic performance. The authors noted, however, that some studies contradict others, making the research hard to interpret. They recommend empowering siblings to be a part of the intervention process, as doing so can have positive effects on the sibling, the child, and the family as a whole.

It is helpful for EI providers to discuss with parents the role of siblings in sessions, as some parents have preconceived notions that they must find child care or alternate activities for their other children so the child with autism can fully benefit from the EI sessions. In the authors' experience, some parents want to exclude siblings from sessions because they think the siblings are disruptive and detract from the learning potential of the session. Some parents have expressed difficulty meeting everyone's needs during the sessions and find having siblings present to be stressful. The authors have found it helpful to begin with parents' comfort level as the parents become familiar with the EI process and learn that the focus is on everyday routines and activities. Many parents who initially exclude other children in the sessions later welcome them and find doing so to be beneficial.

Behaviors of children with ASD can be a significant source of stress for parents (Myers, Mackintosh, & Goin-Kochel, 2009); therefore, an essential part of EI supports may involve teaching parents skills to address challenging behaviors (National Research Council, 2001). Many families have reported to the authors that they limit public outings or trips into the community because they feel judged. The child's "idiosyncratic, unsafe, or disruptive" (Bailey, 2008, p. 319) behavior may result in isolation when families think it is too difficult or too embarrassing to be in public. Decreased interaction with the community can influence the perceived quality of life when families believe others hold judgmental or negative beliefs about a child's disabilities or have difficulty understanding the reasons for the child's behavior (Higgins, Bailey, & Pearce, 2005; Marcus, Kunce, & Schopler, 2005). These feelings of frustration, isolation, and embarrassment are highlighted by one parent's comments about an outing to the park; she remarked, "My child was melting down at the park, taking her clothes off, tantruming on the ground. People stared at us. I had to try to carry her out of the park, half naked and screaming. I could barely carry her, and with her kicking and screaming, it was really hard. Do you think one person said, 'May I help you? Is there anything I can do for you?' No. Not one person offered to help me."

The challenges in parenting a child with ASD or a related disorder may be different from those encountered by parents of typically developing children or those with developmental delays. Typically developing children may have public and private meltdowns, may ignore a parent, may not play or share with other children, may not respect personal space, may get angry, and may refuse to cooperate (Nicholasen & O'Neal, 2008). In children with autism, many of the same behaviors will occur for different reasons and may differ in magnitude from those behaviors experienced by typically developing children. Difficult situations may arise in an ordinary day, as infants and toddlers with autism often present with behaviors including aggression, destruction of property, removal of clothing at inappropriate times, and self-injurious behaviors (Fodstad, Rojahn, & Matson, 2012). Behaviors may be related to some of the core features of autism, such as communication deficits, social deficits, and restricted interests and repetitive behavior (Delmolino & Harris, 2004). At times, parents and providers may perceive a child's behavior through different lenses. For example, one child frequently reached under his mother's and father's glasses and pushed his fingers into their eyes. His mother told the provider, "He worries that we are not happy. He is checking for tears." When it is important that a behavior be changed, it is imperative that all team members be involved not only in determining the function of the behavior but also in the intervention strategies.

In the authors' experience, some families have difficulty setting limits for their children due to fear the children will not understand why they are getting consequences. Many parents have reported that they feel sorry for their child because of the autism and that this made it difficult for them to give developmentally appropriate consequences to commonly occurring behaviors. Providers must respect parents' choices for limit setting, and when appropriate, educate parents as to behaviors that are likely to worsen due to a lack of appropriate consequences. One mother reported she did not want to discipline her son for behaviors including throwing and hitting because she felt badly that he could not communicate in other ways. The provider shared her fears that if the child continued these behaviors he would have difficulty in his upcoming preschool class. This helped the mother understand the need to change her son's behavior, and together, she and the provider devised a plan to help him communicate in ways that would replace the throwing and the hitting.

In some instances, parents attribute behaviors to the child's autism when in fact the behaviors are developmentally appropriate. Behaviors such as biting and screaming are common in neurotypical toddlers, though they may persist longer in young children with autism due to their challenges with social communication. Thus, educating parents on typical development and developmentally appropriate behavior management strategies is another important role for EI providers. These strategies may range from setting up the environment in order to maximize learning and minimize challenging behaviors to implementing procedures to change undesirable behaviors.

The time around the child's transition to preschool can be another source of stress for parents. A child's first school experience is often stressful for parents whether the child is in need of special education or is developing as expected. Parents often wonder about topics such as the student–teacher ratio, the teacher's compassion, the teacher's expertise, the curriculum offered, the child's ability to make friends, and the child's ability to separate. In some cases, the parents have a great deal of difficulty with the separation. When parents have a child with autism, they may also have questions about the child's ability to learn effectively in the classroom, the teacher's level of experience with children who have special needs, the type and amount of therapy provided to meet the child's needs, and the safety of the school as well as transportation provided. In addition, the transition to preschool services affects the parents, as there are often changes in the amount of support provided in the home. As Dicker (2013) stated when discussing moving from infant–toddler services to preschool,

Transition from the rich services of Part C (parent services such as counseling, training, and even respite, an array of child services including nursing, service placement at home or in another natural setting, etc.) to the less generous and school-based programs of Part B for children with ASD has caused major problems. (p. 200)

Families often go from a collaborative process with the EI provider that results in a feeling of confidence and success to feeling anxiety about making the transition to school-based services (Pang, 2010). This process can feel overwhelming for families. EI providers can support families by providing factual information about topics including parental rights, the evaluation process, and the IEP process, ensuring that they support the parents' needs in a way that facilitates collaboration with preschool services. Conversations about transition to preschool should occur in a timely manner, months before a child's third birthday, and should incorporate active listening without judgment or dismissal of their concerns (e.g., "It will be fine").

The stress for families who have children with ASD and related disorders can be overwhelming, and depression may occur. The picture is not entirely fraught with negative experiences, however, as some caregivers cite positive experiences such as gaining a new perspective, growing closer as a family, and attaining personal growth.

Advocacy

In addition to helping families with information about and strategies for facilitating skills and managing behaviors, EI providers are in a position to help families find resources and develop advocacy skills. Resources vary in different communities, and EI providers are often able to help parents investigate respite care, counseling, child care, and community activities. Parents are usually the first to advocate for their child, and it is typical that they continue to advocate for social, financial, educational, and health care supports as the child ages (Ewles, Clifford, & Minnes, 2014; Gensler, 2009). Providers can help parents understand the complexity of their child's ASD and help them navigate various systems and learn terminology associated with each. Effective advocacy involves knowledge of ASD and how it manifests in the child, familiarity with educational guidelines and special education law, and utilization of negotiating and mediating (Bailey, 2008). Though parenting a child with ASD and related disorders can be stressful, many families report positive outcomes such as self-discovery and personal growth as they learn lessons about celebrating small accomplishments and being grateful (Bailey, 2008).

Cultural Considerations and Autism Spectrum Disorder

Cultural factors often influence families as well as the relationship between EI providers and families. It is important that EI providers be sensitive to the significant cultural variation that occurs both between and within cultural groups (Lynch & Hanson, 2011). Families from different cultures have different needs, beliefs, and concerns in response to a child's autism diagnosis and treatment planning (Ennis-Cole, Durodoye, & Harris, 2013; Ravindran & Myers, 2012). Culture may influence what individuals believe about autism (Griffin, Peters, & Smith, 2007). According to Matson et al. (2012), "Symptoms of Autism Spectrum Disorders are universally accepted; however, the reported severity of symptoms may be sensitive to cultural differences" (p. 971).

Providing EI services to families from other cultures necessitates an understanding of culture and also provides opportunities for learning. Travel to their family's birthplace may have an impact on EI services, as some families may go for extended visits and may have concerns about missing sessions or may expect make-up sessions for weeks of missed ones. In some families, a parent or grandparent who lives in the home may leave for extended visits, which can add stress for the parent who remains at home with the young child with autism. In some cultures, extended family may live in the home or stay for extended periods of time. In preparation for her mother-in-law's visit from India, one mother asked the therapist to avoid mentioning autism, saying that she had not mentioned the diagnosis because there was no word for autism in their language.

Cultural factors also affect parents' perceptions, expectations, and interactions. A mother told her EI provider that she thought of her child as "an angel from God, sent to her to do a special job on earth." Another mother, when discussing behavior management strategies, mentioned that she did not know what to do when her son exhibited behaviors such as shaking his drinks so the liquid would splash on his face, scattering cat food, or jumping excessively in his crib. She said she had been physically punished for undesirable behaviors when she was a child growing up in another country, but she knew that would not be acceptable in this country. Some families may feel isolated because of their cultural difference, and having a child with autism may intensify those feelings. Families may isolate themselves, ashamed of the child's atypical development and/or inappropriate behaviors. One mother reported that in India, her birthplace, the doors and windows of the neighboring houses are open, which makes socializing with a child with ASD effortless. She remarked that in the United States, where doors and windows are often shut, she felt isolated by the lifestyle and did not interact with other families due to her child's stereotypy and developmental delays. Because her husband worked long hours and traveled often, the mother reported feelings of isolation and depression.

Hope and Optimism

Research shows that parental feelings of hope and optimism have been correlated with positive outcomes for children with ASD (Bailey, 2008; Durand, 2014). In his book, *Optimistic Parenting,* Durand (2011; see also Durand, 2014) discusses an approach to support families in fostering optimism, which significantly reduces stress and provides hope and help for managing thoughts, attitudes, and beliefs about the child and his or her behavior. Rather than avoiding problems with their children, Durand encourages families to address the problem behaviors directly. When families change their lives to avoid the child's "triggers," flexibility and transitions are not addressed, greatly reducing the child's abilities to cope and adapt in the future. Therefore, one way EI providers can support families is to ask to see the child in routines that are challenging. As a mother told one of the authors, "We can't go outside with him because he will throw a bully fit when we try to come back inside." The author encouraged the mother to consider going outside during sessions so together they could problem-solve solutions to help the child learn skills to make the transition calmly into the house.

EI providers have the capacity to support families in many ways. The authors generated an informal online survey and asked parents about their experiences in EI. Comments regarding the support they received included the following:

"Having someone to help my husband and me navigate the challenge of raising children with special needs. As a parent we often turn to a sibling or mother or mother-in-law to ask advice but raising children with special needs it's almost impossible to ask someone with neurotypical children for advice. It was a huge help and I am forever grateful."

"Just having a calming influence to assure me I was on the right path for my son. Having never needed EI services, having someone point me in the direction was essential for me to gather the courage I needed to move forward regardless of how scared and unsure I was about this new ASD diagnosis."

"Early intervention was invaluable to my son and to us as a family. We learned so many great strategies and felt more hopeful about his future because of the skilled therapy EI provided."

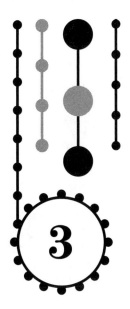

Principles of Behavior and Teaching Strategies

3

Children with autism and related disorders benefit, as do all children, from teaching strategies tailored to their unique strengths and needs. Many of these teaching strategies are derived from principles of behavior. Principles of behavior describe well-researched behavior changes that result from specific interventions; the strategies are practical implementation of the principles. This chapter describes principles of behavior and instructional strategies to help EI providers set up the environment to tailor their intervention to meet the needs of children and families. As aptly stated by Strain et al. (2011), "One could say that we are determining the evidence base of any specific instructional strategy one child at a time. If the current instructional strategy is not yielding the desired outcome, based on the data, then changes to the program must be made" (p. 324). Thus, EI providers should carefully monitor progress to ensure that the strategies being implemented are helping the caregivers and that children gain the skills and behavior changes identified on IFSPs.

TASK ANALYSIS AND SKILL COMPONENTS

Many important daily routines and activities, developmental milestones, and critical skills that infants and toddlers typically master through participation in commonly occurring activities are quite complex and have multiple steps. When a child is having difficulty learning a skill or participating in activities, it is helpful for the EI provider to perform a task analysis and to examine the component skills. A task analysis is a process that examines a skill or activity and breaks it down into its components. For example, Maria's mother, Juanita, would like Maria to play with her kitchen set that she has had for months and ignores except for periodically opening and closing the doors of the microwave and pushing the buttons to make a beeping sound. Maria's EI provider begins to think about the many component skills in playing with a kitchen set. In order to demonstrate this type of play, Maria needs to visually attend to others who cook and/or use her toy kitchen set, she needs to know the function of objects (i.e., how to use a spoon, a cup, a bowl, and a pot), she needs to be able to use her own body to imitate the actions of others, and she needs to sequence actions in play.

One can use a task analysis to teach the parts of a complex activity. For example, imitating stirring involves looking at the person who is stirring, picking up the spoon, placing it in the pot, and moving the spoon in a circular pattern. One can use a task analysis to teach Maria each of these components to imitate stirring, but this skill alone will not help Maria play with her kitchen, as she needs to combine the skill of stirring the pot with other skills such as pretending to add food to the pot and serving the food to others. Maria's mother and EI provider will not only need to look at the skills involved in the play activity, but also will need to consider Maria's motivation when teaching her the steps involved as well as to facilitate Maria's initiation of the activity.

MOTIVATION AND REINFORCEMENT

Motivation is of utmost importance when working with young children with autism and other behavioral challenges. Terrell Bell, the U.S. Secretary of Education during the early 1980s, once said, "There are three things to emphasize in teaching: The first is motivation, the second is motivation, and the third is (you guessed it) motivation" (University of Utah College of Education, 2015). This tenet is applicable to EI, not only for the child, but for the family. When an EI provider who will be providing ongoing services meets a child for the first time, it is important that he or she asks what the child enjoys doing at home and in the community, how he or she entertains him or herself, and which routines go well and which are challenging. In addition, it is imperative to find out what is important to the family so that intervention is targeted to the family's priorities. This information is reflected in the evaluation report and on the IFSP; however, an in-depth discussion with caregivers helps to lay the foundation for EI services. The answers to these questions give a starting point for a myriad of information, including routines in which the provider can embed skill development as well as successes and challenges that exist within the routines. Because child and family needs change over time, it is necessary for providers to have ongoing discussions with families to ensure that priorities are addressed.

In order for new skills and behaviors to be learned, it is necessary to have active participation (Partington, 2008), but obtaining active participation is often challenging when working with young children with ASD. EI providers need to collaborate with parents and other caregivers and analyze what motivates a child to do what he or she does in order to set up opportunities to facilitate learning. By observing a young child during play and other routines, one can determine the infant's or toddler's preferences (e.g., whether the child plays with a toy or object to hear how it sounds, to watch how it moves, to feel or taste it in his or her mouth, and/or to feel it on his or her body). Once knowledge of the child's motivation is gleaned, providers can begin to establish rapport. Terminology for this process varies, and one may find references in the literature to following the child's lead or pairing. Having this knowledge gives the parent and providers ideas for ways to actively engage the child so the adult can be of value to the child.

The following are examples of ways to interact so the child perceives the interactions to be valuable. For children who are difficult to engage, providers may find it helpful to gain their trust by handing them desired items during play and snack time. The objective is to help the child perceive the provider as an ally as opposed to perceiving the provider as someone who only puts demands upon him or her or intrudes into his or her space. Many young children with autism spend a great deal of time activating cause-and-effect toys and electronic items such as phones and tablets. It is often difficult for parents, caregivers, and providers to compete with these items that offer easy access to pleasing sensory features that are extremely predictable. Every time Johnny pushes the icon on the screen, a colorful picture appears along with a sound he finds pleasant. For many children who have difficulty figuring out how to navigate their world, these types of activities often become favorites. A great strategy to use is to *become* a cause-and-effect toy. Using repetitive phrases and gestures and then pausing often evokes a glance and/or a smile that begins the process of establishing rapport. Examples of repetitive activities that are often helpful for an adult to use in establishing rapport include putting an object on his or her head and playfully sneezing, opening and closing the door of a toy car or cupboard, blowing bubbles, or bouncing a ball. Pairing these actions with a sound or word often evokes engagement.

By observing the child and gathering information about what the child likes to do, the provider can help parents and caregivers to develop a list of reinforcers. Reinforcers increase the likelihood that a certain behavior will occur immediately after its presentation. For example, when Joey took his first steps, his parents loudly clapped and cheered. Joey smiled and took another step. His parents' clapping was a reinforcer for his walking. Samantha took her first step and her parents clapped and cheered. She startled, fell to the ground, covered her ears, and screamed. Her parents' loud clapping and cheering was not a reinforcer for Samantha's walking and in fact was a punisher (i.e., something that decreases the future frequency of a behavior that immediately precedes it) for her walking (Cooper et al., 2007). Thus a reinforcer for one child may be a punisher for another.

Gulick and Kitchen (2007) identified five principles that are associated with the effectiveness of reinforcers. The first principle is immediacy, which means the reinforcer must be delivered as quickly as possible after the target behavior occurs. The second principle is contingency, which refers to the need for reinforcers to be provided after the desired response and only that response. Both immediacy and contingency help avoid an undesired behavior from being inadvertently reinforced. For example, Billy's parents praised him and gave him a high-five when he returned his book to the bookcase. They continued to give high-fives, including after he accidentally stepped on his infant sister's hand. He then purposefully stepped on his sister's hand and was surprised when he received a scolding rather than praise. Similarly, Sophia pointed to a cracker and accidentally knocked over her cup, spilling her juice on the table. Her mother handed her a cracker, refilled her cup, and waited for her to point again to a cracker, but instead Sophia dumped her cup and started to scream when she did not get her cracker. The third principle of reinforcer effectiveness is magnitude, which means that the strength of the reinforcer must be sufficient to make the behavior worthwhile. Johnny loved to be tickled, so his father briefly tickled him when Johnny made eye contact during diaper changes. His father noticed that Johnny only made eye contact if he tickled him for over 3 seconds. Variability is the fourth principle of reinforcer effectiveness, because using the same set of reinforcers leads to satiation. Darsh loved small cheese crackers with letters on them, and his grandmother gave them to him every time he came to his highchair when she called him. After a few days, he stopped coming to his highchair when he was called, so his EI provider suggested using a variety of different foods, high-fives, and hugs when he came to his highchair when called, as all of these were favorites. The final principle of reinforcer effectiveness is deprivation, as access to the reinforcement must be limited so the reinforcer keeps its value. Maria's mother attempted to use her phone to entice Maria to sit on the potty, telling her, "First sit and you can play with my phone." Maria's grandmother allowed her to play with her phone throughout the day, so Maria refused to sit on the potty. A strong reinforcer for a child might be a favorite snack food, a favorite toy, or bubbles, but if the child has just eaten lunch, has been playing with the favorite toy all morning, or was popping bubbles for the past 10 minutes, the "reinforcer" will lose its effectiveness and, in fact, will not be a reinforcer at that time. Competing reinforcers in the environment also need to be considered. Tickling and Peekaboo may be great reinforcers when the television is off, but when the child's favorite show is on, these activities may not be important to the child because the television is a stronger reinforcer.

As noted by Leach (2012), in general, natural and social reinforcers are the preferred type of reinforcement to use with young children. A natural reinforcer is the consequence that naturally results from the behavior. For example, if a child points to an item, the natural reinforcer would be obtaining that item. Social reinforcers can include high-fives, praise, hugs, tickles, cheers, or an enthusiastic "yes." These two types of reinforcers, in contrast to gaining access to tangible items or activities unrelated to the target behavior or skill, assist in making the skills meaningful to the child and enhance opportunities for positive social interaction.

A survey such as the Reinforcer Survey provided in Figure 3.1 is a useful tool to assist in determining ways to engage a child as well as to identify possible reinforcers to facilitate skill development. It is helpful to use with families and in child care settings when first meeting a child and to update it as the child's interests change.

REPETITION

Setting up the environment to foster natural opportunities for repetition is extremely beneficial, and many commonly occurring routines and activities in infants' and toddlers' lives provide such opportunities. Early interventionists are in a unique position to help families and caregivers identify repeatable learning opportunities that can be embedded into their days. It is imperative to help families find opportunities that minimize disruptions of the day so as not to induce increased stress on the family. For example, embedding identifying body parts into the bath time routine would not be appropriate to recommend if the family rushes through a bath before taking the child to the babysitter's each morning. The amount of repetition needed varies and is influenced by the child's strengths and needs as well as motivation at a given time. Careful progress monitoring provides feedback to help determine how much repetition is needed before the skill has been mastered.

Using routines offers natural opportunities for repetition. For example, using the routine of diaper changing to facilitate attention to faces can produce about six opportunities in a given day. In addition, some routines such as snack time or mealtime offer opportunities for repeated practice within the routine. For example, during mealtime, a useful strategy may be to place only a few pieces of food on the tray at one time so that the toddler needs to request more. This strategy is appropriate at certain times but not others. For example, if a child is extremely hungry or a parent or caregiver is busy preparing a meal or tending to other children, this strategy would not be appropriate.

SHAPING

Shaping refers to reinforcing behaviors while drawing closer and closer to an end goal. For example, Mohammed was very resistant to drinking from a cup, so his EI provider showed his mother how to start by touching a cup to his lips and giving him a high-five and a cheer. She did this three times and then tipped the cup so a tiny bit of milk touched his lips. Again she cheered and gave him high-fives. His EI provider repeated this several times and then gradually began to tip the cup so a little milk entered Mohammed's mouth. He swallowed the milk and his mother and EI provider cheered and gave him high-fives. Similarly, Jameel's EI provider used shaping to help Jameel progress from grabbing to requesting using his voice. She did this by first allowing Jameel to obtain a piece of cookie from his aunt's hand by grabbing it. After several bites, she told Jameel's aunt to pause before she released the cookie to Jameel. Jameel looked up at his aunt and as soon as he did, the EI provider told her to release the piece of cookie. They repeated this several times, and Jameel learned that when he looked at his aunt, he got his piece of cookie. After several more pieces, the EI provider suggested the aunt wait a few seconds after he looked at her to see if Jameel vocalized to indicate he wanted the cookie. Jameel looked at his aunt, confused as to why he was not getting his cookie, and made a sound as if he were asking a question. The EI provider coached the aunt to model saying "cookie" and give Jameel the bite as soon as he vocalized. After a short period of time, his aunt and the EI provider were able to help shape Jameel's requesting behaviors from grabbing to vocalizing to obtain his pieces of cookie. As his imitation skills improved,

Reinforcer Survey

Directions: This chart lists items and activities that some children enjoy. If your child likes any of these, please add a checkmark under the appropriate column to show how often he or she uses the item or participates in the activity. There is also space for you to add a few of your child's special interests if they are not listed below.

	Never	Rarely	Sometimes	Often	Always
Food and Drink					
Candy					
Chips					
Cookies					
Crackers					
Ice cream					
Juice					
Milk					
Pretzels					
Sensory and Social Play					
Clapping and cheering					
Feeling air blown on (please circle those that are enjoyed) arms, back, belly, legs, head					
Feeling vibrations					
Following siblings					
Imitating or hearing silly sounds					
Jumping					
Massage to (please circle those that are enjoyed) arms, back, belly, head, legs					
Playing chase games					
Playing Peekaboo					
Roughhousing					
Singing					
Swinging (blanket or swing)					
Tickling					
Toys and Activities					
Applying/collecting/looking at stickers					
Blowing bubbles					
Climbing on furniture					
Coloring					
Engaging in messy play					

(continued)

Figure 3.1. Reinforcer Survey.

Figure 3.1. *(continued)*

	Never	Rarely	Sometimes	Often	Always
Looking at books					
Making tents/tunnels					
Putting puzzles together					
Rolling a ball on the floor					
Turning lights on/off					
Turning water on/off					
Using a ring stack					
Using a shape sorter					
Using cause-and-effect toys					
Using modeling dough					
Using toys that spin					
Using smartphone or tablet apps					
Watching television/movies					
Other (please specify)					

they planned to shape the vocalization into the word *cookie*. Shaping involves the use of extinction, which refers to discontinuing reinforcement for a behavior that was previously reinforced (Cooper et al., 2007).

Extinction can be an effective strategy, but there are times when it evokes challenging behaviors. For example, Philip's grandmother gave him crackers whenever he screamed in the grocery store, hoping they would keep him quiet so she could shop without others staring. His screaming increased and grocery trips were very stressful. Philip's aunt, who was studying psychology, told his grandmother she was rewarding his screaming, so the next time they went to the store, his grandmother did not give him crackers. Because in the past screaming led to getting crackers, Philip tried screaming louder and longer, increasing the magnitude of his response, which he thought would likely result in crackers. Philip's grandmother discussed this with the EI provider, who told her this was known as an *extinction burst*. She suggested they go to the store and try giving Philip crackers before he screamed, so his appropriate behavior rather than his screaming would be reinforced.

PROMPTING

Prompting involves providing cues to assist the child to make a desired response. Prompts can be subtle, such as a glance in the right direction when asking "Where's Daddy?" or a change in emphasis when giving a choice such as "Is this milk or juice?" Prompts can also be more apparent or direct, such as guiding the child to ensure the child's response will be accurate. Examples of more apparent prompts include physically guiding a child to pick up an item that was requested or taking him or her to where he or she was directed to go. Many prompts fall in between subtle and very apparent. EI providers must make decisions about when to prompt, what types of prompts to use, and how to decrease or fade prompts during coaching as well as when working directly with a child so that caregivers and the child become independent rather than dependent on prompts.

There are two types of prompt hierarchies, least to most and most to least. Least-to-most prompting involves starting with the least intrusive prompt that will likely result in the desired response, and if that response is not observed, then the next least intrusive prompt is given. Conversely, in most-to-least prompting, a prompt is chosen that will ensure success and then the next least intrusive prompt is chosen. Prompts are most successfully faded when there are sufficient opportunities in a short amount of time. Table 3.1 and Table 3.2 contrast the two types of prompt hierarchies. Table 3.3 exemplifies how physical prompts can be further broken down into partial prompts. Often, most-to-least prompting is a better choice if the skill is new or challenging in order to prevent frustration and unwanted behaviors that often accompany frustration, such as aggression or moving away. Least-to-most prompting is used to increase independence during practice when a child shows emerging abilities to be successful.

Table 3.1. Prompt hierarchy: Least-to-most prompting

Targeted behavior/skill: Laurie will indicate by gesturing that she wants to get down from her booster seat rather than throwing her food or screaming.
When Mom notices that Laurie appears to be finished eating, Mom looks expectantly at Laurie and shrugs as if she is asking a question.
Mom asks Laurie, "What do you want?" when Laurie stops eating but before she screams or cries.
Mom asks Laurie, "Do you want down?" when Laurie stops eating but before she screams or cries.
When Laurie stops eating and appears to be finished, Mom says, "Tell me 'down.'"
When Laurie stops eating and appears to be finished, Mom models by pointing down.
When Laurie stops eating and appears to be finished, Mom takes Laurie's hand and helps her point down, then immediately gets her down.

Table 3.2. Prompt hierarchy: Most-to-least prompting

Targeted behavior/skill: Laurie will walk over to the table and put her cup on it when she is finished drinking.

After Laurie finishes taking a drink,
  Mom walks Laurie over to the table and guides Laurie's hand to place the cup on the table.
  Mom tells Laurie to put her cup on the table.
  Mom asks Laurie, "Where does your cup go?"
  Mom says "table."
  Mom points to the table.

Many children with autism become prompt dependent, and as Leach (2012) points out, this dependency usually is due to a lack of systematically fading the prompts. For example, if Laurie's mother did not fade her prompts and move down the hierarchy as noted in Tables 3.1 and 3.2, Laurie likely would not put her cup on the table unless physically helped or verbally directed, nor would she point down when finished eating unless her mother modeled pointing down or asked her what she wanted. Prompt dependency can also be thought of as responding to a prompt rather than to the cues that are supposed to evoke the desired response or behavior (Cameron, Ainsleigh, & Bird, 1992; MacDuff, Krantz, & McClannahan, 2001).

It is common for EI providers to give children visual supports to help build skills, and it is important that the provider ensures that the visual supports are not interfering with helping the child learn the appropriate natural cue. For example, an EI provider noted that Billy did not say good-bye when she left his home, though he did respond to his mother by saying, "Billy, say good-bye." The EI provider took a picture of Billy waving and suggested that Billy's mother put it on the door and point to it as she told him to wave and say good-bye. Her hope was that Billy would respond to the visual cue rather than to being told what to do. Billy's mother put the picture on the door, and soon Billy was waving and saying good-bye whenever his mother pointed to the picture. Though he was responding to a lower-level prompt on the hierarchy, he was not taught to respond to the natural cue, which was someone saying good-bye. When the EI provider realized this, she quickly changed her tactic and faded the use of the picture by saying "Bye, Billy" while first standing near the picture and, over time, moving so that she blocked more and more of the picture. This resulted in Billy looking at her face, which helped him associate her words and her waving with the needed response.

A similar scenario arose when Anton's mother remarked to his EI provider one day that Anton never said "hi" or "good-bye" appropriately; he only said "hi" and "bye" when told. The EI provider explained that Anton was responding to the prompt to "say hi" instead of saying "hi" when someone said it to him first. During the next session, the EI provider repeatedly left the room and returned playfully and enthusiastically, saying "hi" to Anton's mother, who in return replied "hi" to the therapist with exaggerated affect. After several repetitions, the therapist then included Anton. She said,, "Hi, Mommy," to which Anton's mother responded, "Hi." Then she said, "Hi, Anton," and Anton responded, "Hi" in return. When the therapist returned the next week, Anton's mother proudly remarked that Anton was now greeting his teachers and peers appropriately at preschool.

Table 3.3. Physical prompt hierarchy

Target behavior/skill: When Dad leaves for work and says "good-bye" to Simon, Simon will wave.	
Mom's prompt	Simon's behavior
Mom picks up Simon's hand and waves it.	(Not applicable)
Mom picks up Simon's hand.	Simon waves his hand.
Mom touches Simon's arm.	Simon waves.

GENERALIZATION

It is likely that Anton was able to use his new skill of appropriately responding to "Hi, Anton" because, as his therapist recommended, his mother set up opportunities to practice in the days following the session. She used his stuffed animals and action figures during play routines. In addition, whenever his father or extended family members came into the room, as the therapist had coached her, his mother suggested they say "hi" to Anton and then look expectantly at him in hopes of evoking "hi." Anton was able to generalize this skill because his mother gave him opportunities to respond in a variety of situations with a variety of people.

When children have difficulty generalizing, it is often because they are responding to an aspect of the environment that serves as an unintended signal. For example, at the end of every meal, Landon's mother held up the washcloth and said, "Give me your hand," which Landon quickly did. When the EI provider observed this, she asked Landon's mother to tell Landon "Give me your hand" during other routines to see if Landon followed her direction. At the beginning of the next session, Landon's mother sadly reported that Landon did not follow the direction in the bathtub with her or even in the highchair for his father. The EI provider asked several questions and found out that the washcloth that the mother used in the tub was a different color than the one used at mealtime and that Landon's father used a disposable wipe at mealtime. Landon was responding to the washcloth used at mealtime rather than the verbal direction. Once the provider realized this, she was able to give the family strategies to help Landon respond to the verbal direction. The first step was for Landon's mother and father to use the same color washcloth in a variety of routines so Landon would understand the expectation for him to hold out his hand when told "Give me your hand" in the tub, at the sink, and in the highchair. After a week of successful practice, the EI provider discussed the prompt hierarchy and showed Landon's mother how to fade the visual prompt (i.e., the washcloth) and strengthen the verbal prompt (i.e., "Give me your hand"). The provider coached his mother to tell Landon "Give me your hand" and hold out her hand to signal his response. Landon did not hold out his hand, so the provider suggested moving her hand right next to his; then, Landon gave her his hand. The provider and mother cheered, and Landon smiled. They practiced this with the mother moving her hand a few inches farther from Landon's hand each time, cheering each success, which motivated Landon to continue. After five times, the provider suggested that his mother not hold up her hand. To their delight, when she said, "Give me your hand," Landon held out his hand. The provider suggested that the parents practice "Give me your hand" during other appropriate routines, and if Landon did not hold out his hand, they try the same strategy of fading their hand to help him follow the verbal direction.

COOPERATION, FOLLOWING DIRECTIONS, AND COMPLIANCE

A child's cooperation during routines such as diaper changes and cooperation with following directions such as "give me your cup" or "show me the dog" when looking at books are dependent upon the child's skills, including language comprehension, as well as upon motivation. When a child does not cooperate or follow directions, one must determine if the reason is due to a lack of understanding the direction, a lack of one or more skills required in any of the steps involved in the direction, and/or a lack of motivation. In typical development, toddlerhood is a time of testing limits. Typically, compliance increases over the second and third year (Kopp, 1982). Because of their challenges in understanding language and others' intentions and because of their restricted and repetitive behaviors, young children with ASD often need intervention specifically targeting following directions. Positive behavioral strategies such as the list of tips for toddlers found in Appendix A of the authors' earlier book (Crawford & Weber, 2014) are helpful general approaches that may need to be adapted to assist families. Once children understand "first _____, then _____," known as the Premack principle or Grandma's Law (Cooper et al., 2007), gaining cooperation is much easier. Examples include telling a child "First get your shoes and then we will go outside" or "First sit at the table and then you may have a cookie." Practicing this contingency in a variety of settings and routines with a variety of people helps young children with ASD learn to participate as well as to begin to wait, a difficult challenge for many toddlers.

Behavioral Momentum

Behavioral momentum (Mace et al., 1988) is a technique that often works well to evoke a specific response that is a bit challenging for the child. First, the child is directed to say or do something that is easy for the child and that the parent or provider is relatively certain the child can and will do. The child's correct response is reinforced by praise, a high-five, or other known reinforcer. One or two more easy tasks are presented, and correct responses are reinforced. The next task presented is a little bit harder and, because of the momentum of success, the child is more likely to give the desired response than if the easier tasks were not first completed. This technique works well for practicing new directions to follow in routines. For example, during bath time, when practicing body part identification, Juan's mother implemented this strategy the provider had shown her. She asked him to point to two body parts he knew, his nose and his belly, then clapped and cheered after each one he showed her. He had not yet been consistent in identifying his ears, so next she asked him "Where's your ear?" and then he immediately pointed and clapped for himself.

Determining the Function of Behavior

When children display behaviors that are concerning, such as those that interfere with learning or that affect the well-being of the child or others, it is imperative that the function of the behavior be determined so that an appropriate consequence can be given and a replacement behavior can be taught. Biting, throwing, and hitting are behaviors frequently seen in toddlers, and sometimes, because of communication and social challenges, they tend to persist for longer periods of time in children who have ASD. When a toddlers bites, it may be because he or she is teething, because it worked in the past to get a toy from a peer, or because biting caused Grandma to stop the unpleasant activity of washing the child's face. Each of these scenarios necessitates a different consequence and/or replacement behavior to solve the child's "problem." A child who is teething needs something appropriate to bite. If a child wants something, he or she needs to seek help from another person (e.g., look to an adult or sign or say "help") or to get the item in a developmentally appropriate way (e.g., holding out his or her hand, saying "my turn" or "I want"). If the child cannot have the item, he or she needs to wait or find an alternative. A child trying to escape from getting his or her face wiped needs to communicate "stop" in a more appropriate way, to learn it is not always possible to get what he or she wants, and to accept the imposed touch and interruption of his or her plan that face wiping entails. If behavior strategies are not working, it is often because the function or functions of the behavior were not determined correctly.

A functional behavioral assessment (FBA) is used to determine the function or functions of behavior. This process involves specifically defining the behavior of concern and interviewing caregivers present when the behavior occurs to find out what happens before (antecedents), during, and after (consequences). After the interview, the child is observed and more information is gathered about what happened before, during, and after the behavior. Once the function of the behavior is determined, specific strategies can be developed. For example, the environment may be changed to prevent the behavior from occurring, an appropriate consequence may be recommended, and/or a replacement behavior may be taught. Many states provide resources through their technical assistance agencies to assist with conducting FBAs, and there are many print and electronic resources available. For behaviors that are dangerous or that have more than one function, help may be needed from individuals who have specific training and expertise in conducting FBAs. The function of behaviors is further discussed in the remainder of this book.

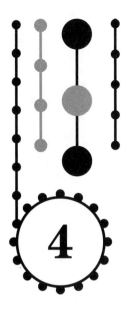

Model for Addressing the Core Deficits of Autism

The model shown in Figure 4.1 addresses the core deficits of autism in infants and toddlers and serves as the framework for Chapters 5 through 8, in which the deficits will be elaborated upon and strategies for intervention will be given. At the base of the triangle are **_Making Sense of Self, Others, and the Environment_** (left) and **_Flexibility_** (right), at the top is **_Social Communication,_** and at the center is **_Regulation_**.

REGULATION

In the literature, the term _regulation_ is used in reference to self-regulation, behavior regulation, and emotional regulation, with no clear distinction between them (Barrett, 2013). In infants, regulation is deeply embedded in the child's relations with others, and establishing connections with caregivers is the first step for the child to learn to manage arousal, sleep–wake cycles, hunger, satiety, self-calming, emotional responsivity, attention, focus, and the capacity to develop homeostasis (DeGangi, 2000; Shonkoff & Phillips, 2000). When an infant or toddler is regulated, he or she is calm, alert, and ready to learn. Conversely, when a young child is tired, hungry, screaming, or avoiding undesirable or aversive sensory stimuli or demands, he or she is not in an emotional state or demonstrating behaviors conducive to relating to others or learning. Thus, regulation affects the ability to be calm and to interact with others, and likewise, the environment affects regulation. Atypical attention, behavioral reactivity, emotional regulation, and activity may compromise the quality and quantity of early social interaction and have been found to be early indicators of autism (Zwaigenbaum et al., 2005).

MAKING SENSE OF SELF, OTHERS, AND THE ENVIRONMENT

When an infant or young child is regulated, he or she is able to interact with others and the environment—the process of Making Sense of Self, Others, and the Environment. Various observable behaviors can be thought of as components of Making Sense of Self, Others, and the Environment, including whether the child attends to sensory stimuli, tolerates sensory stimuli, shifts attention, imitates actions, and follows directions. As infants and toddlers interact with others and their environment, they learn about their bodies through sensorimotor experiences. Infants receive a variety of tactile, visual, auditory, proprioceptive, vestibular, gustatory, and olfactory information from their everyday experiences. They react positively or negatively with facial expressions, sounds, and movement and make associations from repeated experiences. For example,

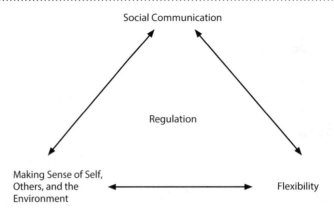

Figure 4.1. Addressing the core deficits of autism spectrum disorder in infants and toddlers.

young infants move their hands to touch toys that are soft and jingle, while cooing and smiling. They turn away from bright lights or the touch of tissues wiping their noses, while fussing, whining, and grimacing. Over time, infants learn to make many sensory and motor associations (e.g., moving their arms results in hitting a toy, which results in tactile, visual, and auditory sensations; feeling hungry results in crying, which results in receiving nourishment; rolling across the room results in a variety of sensations and a method to obtain a desired item). In addition to responding to their physical environment, infants learn quickly about other people in their lives. From young ages, infants look at their caregivers' eyes, return smiles and frowns, and learn to anticipate events from others' actions, sounds, facial expressions, and words that have been repeated during daily routines.

The topic of sensory processing and autism is complicated by multiple theories and varied terminology. There is agreement, however, that atypical responses to sensory information are frequently observed in individuals with ASD (Baranek, Little, Parham, Ausderau, & Sabatos-DeVito, 2014). Baranek et al. describe four sensory features that have been most commonly reported and empirically validated: 1) hyporesponsiveness (i.e., showing decreased reactivity or a delayed response—e.g., not turning to sounds or turning to sounds after an atypical length of time); 2) hyperresponsiveness (i.e., showing exaggerated reactivity or avoidance of sensations—e.g., jerking away from touch); 3) sensory interests, repetitions, and seeking behaviors (e.g., repeatedly licking windows, staring at ceiling fans for extended periods of time); and 4) enhanced perceptions (e.g., hearing a very distant plane, seeing the flickering of fluorescent lights). Children with autism also have difficulties shifting attention between sensory stimuli. In infants with ASD, numerous studies have shown deficits in abilities to look from one object or person to another (Sacrey, Armstrong, Bryson, & Zwaigenbaum, 2014). Hellendoorn et al. (2014) studied atypical visual processing in children with ASD and found that atypical visual behaviors were associated with lower levels of social skills. Similarly, atypical processing of auditory stimuli has been found in individuals with ASD. O'Connor (2012) reported reduced orientation to auditory stimuli, especially speech, in infants, toddlers, and preschoolers. There is little research regarding tactile processing in infants and toddlers with ASD; however, Foss-Feig, Heacock, and Cascio (2012) found in young school-age children a relationship between tactile seeking behaviors (e.g., repeatedly touching certain fabrics, rubbing fingers in saliva) and increased social impairment. In the authors' experience with infants and toddlers with ASD, visual stimuli are often sought after and responded to much more readily than auditory stimuli. Infants and toddlers with ASD frequently, and for excessive amounts of time, watch spinning objects, turn lights on and off, and drop toys to watch them fall.

Temple Grandin (2011), a college professor and author of numerous books about her own experience as an individual with autism, describes engaging in these types of "stimming," or self-stimulatory behaviors, because they feel good and are ways to calm or shut out other stimulation that is painful or uncomfortable. In the authors' experiences, young children with ASD also use repetitive sensory-seeking behaviors when those behaviors result in sensations that are more pleasurable than interactions with others or the environment, when they do not know what else to do, when they are unsure of expectations or demands placed upon them, and/or when they are confused about what is happening in their immediate environment. For example, Billy flicked his fingers in front of his eyes during circle time when he was bored by the story about planets, Jeremy lined up interlocking blocks because he did not know how to put them together, and Rosa flapped her hands in excitement, unable to verbalize "Wow, this is fun." As children are able to better Make Sense of Self, Others, and the Environment and learn new ways to engage with people and objects, they replace repetitive play behaviors such as lining up items, throwing them to hear their sounds, or flicking them for visual stimulation with more typical play and interaction.

FLEXIBILITY

Once a child begins to understand the world through repeated experiences and starts to make associations, he or she begins to make predictions and then learns that those predictions do not always materialize. The ability to accommodate to these changes constitutes Flexibility. For example, an infant cries when hungry, and then his or her parent appears with a bottle. Over time, the infant learns that crying results in someone bringing a bottle and later expects a bottle when he or she cries. As time goes on, he or she learns that there are variations within this rule that crying results in a bottle. The temperature of the liquid may change, the taste of the liquid may change, the person holding the bottle may change, the location where the bottle is given may change, and/or the look of the bottle may change.

Individual differences in sensory processing (hypersensitivity and hyposensitivity) and temperament as well as responses of caregivers influence Flexibility. For example, Mary's, Julie's, and Sophie's mothers routinely warmed their daughters' bottles, until one day at their playgroup they learned that many young toddlers drink their bottles cool or cold. The next day, the mothers gave their daughters cooler formula. Mary and Julie took one sip and promptly threw their bottles and cried. Sophie took a sip of hers, grimaced, and sucked again, adapting without difficulty. Mary's mother immediately warmed the bottle and continued to do so for the next several weeks but forgot to tell a babysitter about this preference. When the babysitter gave Mary her bottle, Mary threw it and cried. The babysitter thought Mary was not hungry and presented the cold bottle an hour later. Mary was so hungry that she fussed a little but then drank the bottle. Julie's mother decided to warm Julie's bottle less and less over time so Julie would have an easier time. Each child adapted to the change; however, sensory preferences, temperament, and caregiver responsivity influenced the process.

Adapting to changes is necessary for Regulation, interaction, and learning new skills. All daily routines necessitate adapting to changes in the physical environment, changes in routines, changes in caregivers, and changes in responses of others. Children with ASD often have difficulty with Flexibility, and changes in routines affect their Regulation. A child may cry or have a tantrum when there is a change in schedule or a variation in a routine such as taking a different route to a familiar place. It is well documented that individuals with ASD have trouble adapting to demands of the environment, show rigid behavior, hold on to previous behavior patterns, have restricted and repetitive behaviors, have a strong preference for behavioral and environmental consistency, and show difficulty in adapting to changes in plans or alterations in daily routines (D'Cruz et al., 2013; Kanner, 1943; Kenworthy, Case, Harms, Martin, & Wallace, 2010). Though repetitive behaviors are common in typical development, Wolff et al. (2014) found that children who were later diagnosed as having ASD had a broad range and increased frequency of repetitive behaviors as early as 12 months of age. Restricted and repetitive behaviors seem to be closely related to challenges with cognitive flexibility, which involves planning, working memory, impulse control, inhibition, and initiation (Yerys et al., 2009). According to Deák (2004), flexible cognition involves "adapting inference to unfamiliar or unexpected situations, creatively combining concepts, and modifying familiar knowledge and habits to produce novel representational syntheses or action sequences" (p. 272). Pretend play, a milestone in the early years, involves such a synthesis. This use of knowledge and skills can also be thought of as generalization, or the application of skills in new situations. These skills, which typically begin to develop in the preschool years (Gillis & Nilson, 2014), are needed for successful participation in routines at home and in the community throughout the life span.

SOCIAL COMMUNICATION

Not only do young children need to attend to and appropriately respond to their environment and its changes, they also need to interpret and respond to the actions and words of the people around them. This process of interpreting and responding describes Social Communication. Although there is no generally accepted definition of social communication, according to Bruner (1981), social communication has three functions: social interaction, behavior regulation, and joint attention. Bottema-Beutel, Yoder, Woynaroski, and Sandbank (2014) discussed how all communication is social in nature because it involves at least two people, and they distinguished between communication that is for the purpose of relating to others and communication for the purpose of regulating others' behavior, such as requesting an item. In their research, they limited their definition to communication that is directed to another person, is primarily to share affect or interest, is not merely imitative, and is not a response to a prompt or question. The American Speech-Language-Hearing Association (ASHA) uses Adams's (2005) definition of social communication: "the synergistic emergence of social interaction, social cognition, pragmatics (verbal and nonverbal), and receptive and expressive language processing" (p. 182); however, the information on ASHA's web page is limited to school-age children, and resources regarding younger children have not been developed at the time of this writing (ASHA, 2015c). ASHA (2015a) has an online resource that cites social interaction, social cognition, pragmatics (both nonverbal and verbal), and language processing as components of social communication. (These terms and components are further discussed in Chapter 8.) In addition, ASHA (2015b) provides a list of social communication benchmarks from infancy to adulthood that includes a wide variety of expressive and receptive language skills.

In infants and toddlers, Social Communication begins with one or two exchanges of engagement and progresses to multiple exchanges that exemplify early conversation skills. Skills that are necessary to move from engagement to reciprocal social communication (explored in depth in Chapter 8) include looking into others' eyes; imitating gestures, sounds, and words; using gestures for a variety of functions; using words for a variety of functions; and participating in multiple exchanges with gestures and/or words. Joint attention is also an important component of Social Communication. Schertz and Odom (2007) defined *joint attention* as "visually coordinating attention with a partner to an external focus, showing social engagement and an awareness of the partner's mutual interest for the purpose of 'commenting' rather than 'requesting'" (p.1562). There are two types of joint attention: responding to joint attention (RJA) and initiating joint attention (IJA). RJA refers to the behavior of looking or looking and pointing that an individual exhibits in response to another person doing the same. For example, Sumina saw that her mother was looking out the window, so she also looked. IJA refers to behavior an individual exhibits when he or she shifts gaze, with or without a gesture, in order to shift someone else's attention (Bruinsma, Koegel, & Koegel, 2004). Joshua demonstrated this when he looked at his cup that had spilled, looked at his mother, and glanced back to his cup to show his mother the mess. Joint attention, which typically begins to develop at the end of the first year, is considered a precursor to verbal skills and a precursor to social responsiveness (Schertz, Odom, Baggett, & Sideris, 2013).

Because Social Communication is considered to be a core deficit in ASD, intervention that specifically targets Social Communication has been the focus of much research (Anagnostou et al., 2015). Bottema-Beutel et al. (2014) reviewed interventions that targeted Social Communication outcomes for preschoolers with ASD and found representation of developmental, behavioral, pragmatic, and sensory-based theories in the approaches with the best empirical support. In addition, Bottema-Beutel and colleagues noted that these approaches "incorporate child preferences, responsive interventionists who encourage shared control of interactions and offer meaningful reinforcement, sequenced goals that reflect the child's developmental level, and an understanding of the family's current functional needs" (p. 808). The framework depicted in Figure 4.1 also incorporates developmental, behavioral, pragmatic, and sensory-based theories and targets Social Communication.

PUTTING IT TOGETHER

In summary, the model shown in Figure 4.1 emphasizes the relationship between Regulation; Making Sense of Self, Others, and the Environment; Flexibility; and Social Communication. Regulation is at the center because Regulation is necessary for Making Sense of Self, Others, and the Environment as well as for Flexibility and for Social Communication. Making Sense of Self, Others, and the Environment leads to Flexibility. When a child exhibits Flexibility, he or she can then Make Sense of Self, Others, and the Environment. This foundation leads to the ability to communicate; through communication, more is learned about Self, Others, and the Environment. In addition, Making Sense of Self, Others, and the Environment; Flexibility; and Social Communication assist with Regulation. Wetherby (1991) captures these relationships in her statement, "The child's behavior influences the caregiver's responsiveness which influences the child's development. The child's developmental outcome is determined by the mutual interaction or transaction of the child and the environment" (p. 255). In addition, one can conclude that EI providers have enormous potential to have an impact on parents and other caregivers and their children by supporting them through these processes that occur in the early years.

The following vignette illustrates how the framework presented applies to infants and children who exhibit red flags for autism or who have a diagnosis of ASD. Sabrina, age 24 months, was referred to EI by her pediatrician due to concerns of delayed communications and infrequent eye contact. The pediatrician administered the M-CHAT-R and discussed the results with the family. Sabrina received an EI evaluation, which showed significant delays in all areas of development. Her physical skills were functional, but because she did not imitate, it was difficult to engage her in structured activities, and it was difficult to determine her true abilities. The concerns Sabrina's parents identified included frequent tantrums when they interrupted her for diapering, dressing, mealtime, or getting into the car. During tantrums, Sabrina frequently kicked and hit. Her parents also said that both Sabrina and they felt frustration because they seldom knew what she wanted. The only time they knew what she wanted was when she stood in front of the refrigerator and banged on the door so they would get her a bottle. Her parents had tried to take her hand to use the sign for milk that they saw in a book, but when they took her hand she screamed and hit them. After she would drink her bottle, she threw it on the floor, and if she wanted more she ran to the refrigerator and banged on it, screaming until her parents came to give her more milk. If they did not give her more, she swiped her arm along the counter, causing items to crash to the floor. Her parents repeatedly told her she could have more milk later, but she did not seem to understand. Sabrina's parents said that they knew she was really smart because she knew her letters and numbers. They believed she recognized colors because she refused to drink out of any bottle unless it had a yellow ring that held the nipple. Her parents expressed frustration because Sabrina did not seem connected to them. She preferred to play by herself and seemed to dislike them: every time they tried to play with her, she moved away to flip pages in a book, lick the window, or drop toys behind the toy box.

Sabrina's IFSP outcomes focused on helping Sabrina communicate her wants and needs and increasing her interactions with her parents throughout daily routines. Sabrina's EI provider focused on coaching Sabrina's parents in Regulation; Making Sense of Self, Others, and the Environment; Flexibility; and Social Communication. In the first few weeks of services, in the area of Making Sense of Self, Others, and the Environment, the EI provider taught Sabrina's parents to playfully use songs and sensory-social games, pausing and quickly resuming them when Sabrina looked at their eyes. This taught Sabrina that good things happened when she demonstrated eye contact. The sensory-social games included many that involved movements and touch so Sabrina would learn that people taking her hands potentially resulted in fun. Later, her parents learned to pause during "Row, Row, Row Your Boat" and tickle games and to wait until Sabrina pulled their hands towards her body before continuing the game. Through this process, Sabrina learned more about using her body to control the actions of others, which resulted in increasing her Regulation and readiness to be engaged with others.

The EI provider helped the family learn to better recognize Sabrina's cues when she was getting tired of a game or when she wanted more. The parents learned that reading her cues also assisted with her Regulation, as she was less likely to have a tantrum. To help Sabrina's abilities in Making Sense of Self, Others, and the Environment—specifically, making sense of others' actions such as when her parents were taking her to the changing table and the car—the EI provider taught the family to give Sabrina visual cues. They showed her a diaper to signal it was time for a diaper change, their keys to signal it was time to get in the car, and her shoes to signal it was time to go outside. Sabrina's parents learned to give her other visual cues to help her understand the many transitions that occur in any given day. This strategy greatly reduced her tantrums, and her parents reported an increase in Sabrina's Flexibility. Flexibility was also incorporated into the sensory-social routines, as the EI provider showed the family ways to vary the songs and games very gradually. They also worked on Flexibility by targeting Sabrina's bottle drinking by gradually changing the color of the rings using colored markers and ribbon until she easily drank from a variety of bottles.

The EI provider also showed Sabrina's parents how to encourage Sabrina's Social Communication. When Sabrina went to the refrigerator and banged on it, her parents put their hands toward the handle of the refrigerator and paused. Sabrina pushed their hands toward the handle and they then opened the door. Again they paused and she pushed their hands toward the milk. The EI provider coached her parents how to shape Sabrina's communication from banging on the refrigerator to pulling them to the refrigerator. To help Sabrina accept the limit of being told that she could not have more milk or that it was not time for milk, the EI provider suggested putting a picture of her bottle on the refrigerator door when milk was available to her. Sabrina learned that if the picture was on the door her parents gave her milk and that when the picture was absent her communication attempts resulted in her parents' telling her "no milk." Over time, this visual cue assisted in Sabrina's Making Sense of Self, Others, and the Environment, and her counter clearing when she could not have milk disappeared.

Sabrina's parents began to experiment and found that when Sabrina was happy and regulated, they were able to engage her in new experiences. During these times, they were able to set up situations to encourage her to communicate by taking their hands and by moving her body to indicate that she wanted more of a tickle game or a song. On days when she was irritable, they learned to expect the skills she had mastered, but to keep her regulated, they avoided trying to teach her new skills. Sabrina's parents found that they frequently moved from Making Sense of Self, Others, and the Environment to Flexibility and to Social Communication, looking for signs of Regulation to help Sabrina throughout the day. In the next months, the EI provider was able to introduce imitation, following directions, and handing items to others to obtain help in a variety of routines. When Sabrina's service coordinator visited after 3 months of services, the parents were thrilled to show her the new skills they had learned. They reported fewer tantrums and expressed gratitude that their daughter was interacting with them in a variety of ways.

Sabrina's story illustrates strategies this chapter introduced to facilitate Regulation; Making Sense of Self, Others, and the Environment; Flexibility; and Social Communication. These strategies, along with the principles of behavior and teaching strategies discussed in Chapter 3, are integrated in Chapters 5 through 9 so EI providers can help families like Sabrina's address the core deficits of ASD during daily routines with their infants and toddlers.

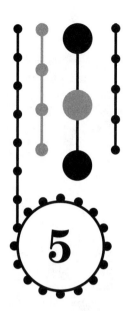

Building Skills to Support Regulation

5

The term *regulation* is used in a variety of fields, including psychology, infant mental health, occupational therapy, education, and speech-language pathology. Clear definitions and boundaries are difficult to ascertain among the constructs of behavior regulation, emotional regulation, and self-regulation, as theorists and researchers use terminology specific to their fields and frames of reference. This chapter presents a synthesis of literature as well as its relevance to young children with autism and related disorders.

Regulatory processes begin to develop prenatally and can be seen in differences in responses of newborns to sensory stimuli of certain intensities (Calkins, 2007). These varying responses are related to a child's temperament, the biologically based individual differences in mood, emotion, attention, and motor reactivity or response that are dependent on situations and influenced by genetics, environment, and experience (Mazefsky et al., 2013; Rothbart & Bates, 2006; Rothbart, Posner, & Kleras, 2006). Temperament constructs include affect, surgency, and effortful control. The construct of affect can be understood by examining its continuum. On one end of the continuum is the tendency to be fearful, easily frustrated, and irritable, and at the other end lies the tendency to be laid back and adaptable. Similarly, surgency can be explained by its continuum, with the tendency to be shy, inhibited, and withdrawn on one end and the tendency to actively and energetically approach others in a positive manner on the other. Effortful control's continuum is marked by the inability to regulate arousal in order to remain calm and focused on one end and the ability to sustain attention, control one's own behavior, and regulate one's own emotions on the other (Rothbart & Bates).

Responsive caregivers are able to modulate infants' arousal and mood by exciting or calming them, which is how Muratori, Apicella, Muratori, and Maestro (2011) define regulation. Others have used the terms *co-regulation* (Fogel, 1993) and *mutual regulation* (Gianino & Tronick, 1988) to describe this process. Casenhiser, Shanker, and Stieben (2013) described co-regulation as follows:

> The natural, perhaps instinctive, effect of one person's arousal level on another person's arousal level. It is the mechanism that accounts for the phenomenon that is observed in an interaction when one person's whispering causes the other person to also start whispering. It is the mechanism by which a mother soothes an upset child by speaking slowly and softly. In a sense, a person's arousal level can be thought of as contagious. (p. 224)

At first, parents or other primary caregivers are responsible for maintaining regulation by attending to and acting upon infants' changes in alertness and comfort and learning to read cues to keep their young children calm and content. Parents often use visual, auditory, tactile, and movement distraction in order to shift infants' attention to calm and soothe them. They soothe distress, avert fear, and foster positive emotion as they help their infants manage their emotions (Thompson & Meyer, 2014). Between the ages of 3 and 6 months, infants and caregivers begin reciprocal exchanges of smiles and attention that foster regulation. Infants also use gaze aversion to reduce their stress when overstimulated or uncertain (Repacholi, Meltzoff, Rowe, & Toub, 2014). During the next 6 months, infants learn to initiate responses from a parent using behaviors such as calling for attention or raising the arms to be picked up (Sroufe, 2000). They also are able to use their motor skills to approach what they desire or escape from what they do not want, both of which assist them to regulate. During the second year of life, young children also begin to regulate using the social cognitive skills of gaze following, social referencing, and imitating the emotions of others (Repacholi et al.). Also during this time, toddlers' vocabularies increase and, as shown by Vallotton and Ayoub (2011), language skills help regulate behavior. Thus, as infants and toddlers grow and mature, they are able to regulate their own motor and affective behavior and gain control over impulses and actions as determined by situations to become behaviorally compliant and to delay gratification (Calkins, 2007). This leads to self-regulation, the ability to modulate one's reactivity to internal and external stimuli at a level appropriate for one's age and temperament. Self-regulation involves emotional control, behavioral strategies, and cognitive strategies including attention and planning (Henrichs & Van den Bergh, 2015).

In a study of more than 14,000 children in Great Britain, researchers found that persistent regulatory challenges in sleeping, eating, and crying predicted dysregulated behavior across childhood. Children with three areas of dysregulation at 15–18 months had the highest degree of dysregulation throughout their childhood. Excessive crying was the largest predictor of dysregulation across time (Winsper & Wolke, 2014).

One can see that Regulation both affects and is affected by caregiver interaction, sensory processing, and communication. For young children with autism, because of their challenges in Making Sense of Self, Others, and the Environment, in Flexibility, and in Social Communication, Regulation often is a significant need. Challenges with Regulation can affect any daily routine and can manifest as temper tantrums that may begin as frustration and then lead to avoidance and escape behaviors (Konst, Matson, & Turygin, 2013). Frustration may arise from skill deficits, such as a lack of understanding about what is expected or what comes next, or from an inability to communicate. In addition, infants and toddlers often get frustrated because they do not have the physical abilities to do what they want (e.g., activating toys, putting together toys, manipulating figures into poses). According to Deborah Lipsky (2011), a woman who was diagnosed with autism as an adult, many individuals with autism use repetitive self-stimulatory behaviors to calm or regulate themselves and reduce anxiety. Anxiety often occurs when something unexpected happens, and the repetitive behaviors help the individual find predictability, which serves as a calming mechanism. In the authors' experience, a common challenge occurs when a child "stims" and misses many opportunities to engage with others and play appropriately. Brianna is a child who stimmed on straws, pencils, and other long, thin objects she could find, flicking them and watching intently as they moved back and forth. Whenever she saw a cup with a straw, she darted to it, which made it challenging for her family to go to restaurants, amusement parks, and other places where straws are common. At home, her parents were very busy taking care of Brianna and her siblings and found it much easier to let Brianna stim than to hear her scream when they took away the item she was flicking near her eyes. She did not entertain herself well and was not as happy as when she had her pencil or straw, and her parents wanted her to be happy. Her EI providers discussed how this behavior interfered with learning and also supported the parents by discussing how they understood that sometimes parents must prioritize to get through the day. They offered to help Brianna's parents work on strategies to help her find more appropriate ways to get her sensory needs met and to help her learn to regulate herself when she did not have an item on which to stim.

In their efforts to reduce dysregulation such as screaming, aggression, or head banging that occur when their children are exposed to sensations they perceive as unpleasant, when they are unable to communicate their wants and needs, when they are enjoying what they are doing and someone stops them, and/or when they do not know what is happening, parents often find themselves helping the child calm himself or herself in that moment, which inadvertently strengthens the challenging behavior. For example, Jamal's mother gave him his milk in the blue cup because the green one he used every day was not yet washed. Jamal screamed and banged his head on the floor, mad that he did not have his usual cup and unable to say he wanted the green one. His mother was afraid he would hurt himself, so she quickly washed the green cup and gave it to him. Jamal immediately stopped banging his head on the floor. When his cup was empty, he threw it and immediately began to bang his head, frustrated that his cup was empty and unable to communicate that he wanted more. His mother quickly gave him more milk. Jamal realized he had found a new communication tool: he banged his head and his needs were quickly met. This chain of events and behaviors can occur with any child, but because of the core deficits of ASD, these challenges often continue for greater lengths of time.

In order to address regulatory issues, one must do an analysis to determine if the cause is due to challenges with Making Sense of Self, Others, and the Environment; Flexibility; and/or Social Communication. This will help providers and families develop strategies that may include modifying the environment and teaching replacement behaviors. In Jamal's case, the EI provider who witnessed the tantrums during her first session formulated a plan to address Jamal's communication skills, including shaking his head or saying "no," pointing, and handing items to others for help. She knew it would take some time before Jamal would be able to use these skills, and she knew that one of her first goals would be to help Jamal's family manage his tantrums so he would be safe and so they would not inadvertently reinforce his undesirable behaviors.

In addition, the EI provider knew that once children with ASD learn the power of their communication, they are often confused when their communication strategies do not yield results as they did in the past. When a child first points to a desired item or says the name of the item, parents, caregivers, and EI providers are thrilled and typically reinforce the child's efforts. The child then learns that using gestures and words results in the requested items. For example, Rebecca began to use a variety of communication strategies, including pulling her mother to the refrigerator and pointing to items inside to indicate what she wanted. She also began to hand her mother the remote to indicate that she wanted to watch television. A few days later, Rebecca took her mother to the refrigerator and pointed to pudding for the third time that day. Her mother told Rebecca "no pudding," and Rebecca had a meltdown. Rebecca did not understand why the rule had changed and did not understand her mother's reasons for not giving her the pudding. She had learned her communicative powers and then the power was revoked, causing confusion and frustration. Another common cause of dysregulation in children with autism is having to wait to have their needs met. Sometimes this is because the act of waiting is difficult, whereas other times the dysregulation is due to difficulties interpreting others' intentions. For example, a child may not understand that when the caregiver walks away, the caregiver is in the process of getting a drink or something to eat or otherwise meeting a need.

Many EI providers and parents use sensory strategies to help young children regulate. A quiet voice, rocking, massaging, and hugging are commonly used to sooth infants and toddlers. In addition, some EI providers recommend equipment such as brushes, weighted vests, pressure vests, and weighted blankets. When recommending strategies to help a child regulate, it is important to ensure that the strategies are not reinforcing unwanted behaviors. For example, whenever Abdul started to dump his toys, his mother gave him a big hug and he stopped dumping the toys. Over time, Abdul's toy dumping increased, as he discovered this was a great way to get his mother's attention when she was on the phone, cooking, or otherwise occupied. Though he was calm after a hug, he had learned it was a fast way to get attention.

Some EI providers recommend weighted vests or lap pads to help children sit at circle time in child care or preschool settings. It is important that data be taken both with and without the weighted products across several opportunities in order to objectively determine if the products are affecting the targeted behavior. For example, Joseph's team members decided to determine whether Joseph would stay at circle time longer when he wore a weighted vest. During circle time, they timed how long Joseph stayed with the group and found he stayed at circle time for 5 minutes, 3 minutes, and 7 minutes on three different days when he was wearing a weighted vest and for 2 minutes, 8 minutes, and 5 minutes on three other days when he was not. When they averaged the data, they found no difference. His team then began to think about factors that may have been affecting Joseph's ability to stay at circle time and realized Joseph did not understand much of what was discussed at circle time and that this greatly affected his ability to sit and participate. In the authors' experience, many children who have difficulty sitting at circle time struggle because of the complexity of the language, which makes many circle time activities lack meaning. It is important for EI providers to make recommendations to increase a child's physical participation, such as sitting with the group, but also to make recommendations to make activities more meaningful for the child. For example, EI providers should look at where the child sits relative to the teacher to help the child maintain attention and also should make recommendations regarding the use of objects, gestures, signs, and/or pictures, depending on the child's needs at that time, to aid in the child's language comprehension. In addition, using music and preferred sensory activities as part of circle time often help a child participate. Brainstorming with team members about the child's strengths and challenges while looking at the demands of the activity can lead to accommodations that foster increased regulation, participation, and learning.

Many times, parents who have young children with autism have to work very hard to achieve the desired responses of having children "do what they are told." Each family has its own set of rules; some families tend to be lenient and others tend to be strict. In the authors' experience, in terms of Regulation, more important than the number of rules is the consistency with which the rules are enforced. For many reasons, parents often give young children several chances to stop undesirable behavior or to follow directions and are not always consistent in their rules and expectations. Some parents are not aware of the importance of consistency, whereas others are but struggle to get through each day and do not have the energy to make changes in how they approach their children's behavior challenges. For young children with autism, this lack of predictability can be very confusing and can often be the cause for dysregulation. Parents have reported that it is difficult to implement common behavior management strategies for their children with autism or related disorders because they feel sorry for them and/or because they feel their children will not understand. In addition, some families attempt to make changes and may not understand that, often, challenging behaviors get worse before they get better due to extinction bursts, as discussed in Chapter 3. Some parents who know about extinction bursts may not have the support and resources to assist their child. Many parents "put up" with behaviors such as screaming and aggression until they reach a point when they are ready to work on them. At times, EI providers find it challenging to "meet the family where they are" and also to help them understand the importance of changing challenging behaviors when children are very young. Several parents who have older children have offered the authors advice to give parents with young children, including, "If you don't want him to do it in public, don't let him do it at home," "As the child gains skills make sure you expect more," "Don't enable manipulative behavior," and "It is important to get behavior under control when the child is young. It only gets harder when the child is older." The authors have found it helpful to introduce discussions regarding changing challenging behaviors if the parents have not done so and to let the parents know that if and when they would like support to make those changes, the provider can assist them.

When the family requests help to change behaviors and EI providers are ready to help, it is imperative that the provider have an open mind as to the possible causes of the behaviors and to look at the behavior from the child's perspective as well as the adults'. For example, 28-month-old Maya's grandmother reported during Maya's evaluation that Maya hated to be in the highchair and would not sit for meals. Her grandmother reported that Maya would eat only if allowed to run around. Her grandmother had to shampoo the carpet weekly because Maya made such a mess. The evaluator hypothesized that Maya may not like the feeling of being confined in the highchair and asked whether Maya sat in the car seat, grocery cart, and stroller. Maya's grandmother reported that Maya was fine during those routines, so the evaluator asked more questions and found out that Maya was fine in the highchair until Maya's grandmother turned to walk to the refrigerator to get her food, at which point Maya started to scream. The evaluator wondered whether Maya was having difficulty waiting for the food because she did not understand that her grandmother was going to get it and/or whether Maya was not yet able to wait to get her needs met. The evaluator suggested they try an experiment and have Maya's food ready on her tray before putting her in her highchair. When her grandmother brought her to her highchair and showed her the food, Maya cooperated, getting in the highchair and calmly eating her food.

The remainder of this chapter presents common challenges with Regulation observed during daily routines, possible reasons that they may occur, and strategies to prevent or control them. Subsequent chapters present strategies to facilitate Making Sense of Self, Others, and the Environment; Flexibility; and Social Communication. EI providers can present these strategies to families to help the child more easily participate in routines; the language used is that which an EI provider would say to parents and caregivers in order to coach and support them. As discussed, building these skills will assist with Regulation. In addition, there are many strategies that can be used to prevent dysregulation as well as ones that help foster Regulation when a child is upset.

Tips and Hints that Cross Multiple Routines to Prevent Dysregulation

Many times children have several behaviors that parents would like to change. It is important to prioritize and limit the number of behaviors addressed simultaneously so the child and the caregivers are not overwhelmed.

Be as consistent as possible with rules and expectations. If a child is given a random number of chances before a consequence is given, the child never knows if and when there will be follow-through. When the child does get a consequence, he or she may have a tantrum or be dysregulated due to the lack of predictability. In addition, the inconsistency of the consequence strengthens the undesirable behaviors. The following sequence will help children follow directions with which they can be physically helped: 1) gain the child's attention, 2) give the direction and if the child does not comply, repeat the direction, 3) repeat the direction again, followed by "or I will help you." If he or she does not follow the direction, help the child to do so.

Give directions stating what to do rather than what not to do. For example, instead of "Stop jumping on the couch," tell the child "Get down" or "Jump on the floor."

Thinking about the child's understanding of cause and effect, safety, and impulse control, try to anticipate what could be a problem and redirect before a tantrum occurs. Consider whether the behavior is something that the child will likely outgrow and, if not, consider whether it will be acceptable in a year or two.

Give warnings that use consistent, simple language, such as "It's almost time to ____. I'll count to 10, then it's time to _____."

Some children respond well to "bye-bye ___" or "all done ___" to cue them that there is a change. For example, when Jimmy was playing with a truck at the store and his mother was ready to leave the toy aisle, his mother said, "Bye-bye truck. See you next time."

Use relevant songs, objects, pictures, gestures, or signs to aid with comprehension during transitions. Examples include singing a clean-up song, showing a food item to a child who is playing and walking with it to the table saying, "Time for snack"; using a hand-washing gesture and saying, "Time to wash hands"; or showing a photo of the child in the tub and saying, "Time for bath." Children who do not understand abstract representations will need to learn the meaning of the cues before the cues will be useful. Similarly, picture schedules and "first–then" pictures only assist with transitions when children understand their meaning. Acquiring meaning may take quite a bit of practice.

Focus on what the child will be doing next rather than what the child is leaving, making the new activity seem as desirable as possible. For example, when it is time to leave the playground, after giving a warning and saying good-bye to the slide or the activity in which the child is engaged, tell him or her, "Let's go get your _____," referring to a preferred item such as a cup, snack, or toy that was left in the car.

Give choices when appropriate, such as "You can't have a cookie, but you may have a cracker or a banana." For children who have difficulties with language, show them the choices.

Pay a lot of attention to desired behaviors and as little as possible to undesirable ones. For example, if a child is able to communicate using gestures and/or words but tends to scream at times, responding quickly and enthusiastically to appropriate communication and ignoring screaming will likely increase the appropriate communication and decrease the screaming.

Be very clear to differentiate what is a choice and what is a direction. Choices are questions and begin with "will you," "do you want to," "can you," or statements that are followed by "okay?" all of which give the child the option to say or show that the answer is no. Directions, on the other hand, are statements that are expected to be followed. For example, Molly's mother said, "Molly, it's time to leave for school, okay?" Molly said no and then became very upset when her mother picked her up to take her to the car to leave, as she believed she was given the option to stay home.

When young children have a tantrum because they cannot have something they want, many parents and caregivers offer them something else they can have. This strategy often works when children are very young, but as they get older, it does not and often results in aggressive behavior such as hitting or throwing the alternative item. Often, presenting two options rather than just one works well, as the children feel they have more control.

Many times, young children who have autism are very self-directed and have a tantrum or walk away when others try to engage them in an activity. Positive reinforcement, such as praise or a sensorimotor reward, and shaping (as described in Chapter 3) often work well. Other times, however, the child may benefit from using "One time, then done," whereby the child is helped to do the activity and then he or she is allowed to do what he or she wants for several minutes before the demand is again presented. Over time, the child is helped less and less until he or she is performing the task independently.

Many young children often request to go outside, to watch television, to eat a snack, or to play an app on a tablet or a smartphone and become upset when they cannot have what they want. They are unable to predict when they will or will not have access to these pre-ferred items, and when denied, they often will have a tantrum. Their access to these items and activities is often perceived as random, and the unpredictability adds to the confusion. Placing a large, laminated X on a television, a door, a refrigerator, or a cupboard to signify that it is off-limits can be helpful. The child will not understand its significance at first, but will learn that the X signifies "not now." It is important that the X be removed when the child has access to the opportunity *before* the child makes the request. This is because if the child goes to the television and the parent takes the X off and then turns on the television, the child will think that going to the television resulted in the removal of the X. The next time the child goes to the television and the X stays, he or she will likely become dysregulated, and thus the X did not serve its purpose.

Many times, adults will ignore a child who is communicating that he or she wants something that the child cannot have, hoping the child will give up. For a child with communication challenges, the child does not know whether the adult understood the request and tends to be very insistent, just in case the message was not received. It is recommended that the child is told "No ___ now. All done ____" so the child knows he or she was understood. The child will likely be upset that he or she cannot have the desired item; however, the child will likely calm more quickly knowing that the message was received.

Make routines the child resists such as nose wiping, toothbrushing, and hair rinsing as pre-dictable as possible. At the beginning of the routine, tell the child what will be happening and, if needed, show the child the tissue, the toothbrush, or other item that identifies the rou-tine so he or she knows what will be happening. In addition, make the ending predictable by singing a song that ends when the routine ends or counting to 10 and always stopping at 10. Vary the speed of the song or counting so that its ending occurs at the same time as the dis-liked activity. In addition, the use of phrases such as "almost done" and "quick, quick, quick" provide predictability by cueing the child that the duration of the disliked routine is short.

When something unpredictable happens, such as when blocks fall as the child is building, use humor and emphatically say, "Oh, man." Over time, many children will begin to use this phrase rather than getting upset in similar disappointing situations.

Various strategies can be implemented to help children learn to wait. Turn-taking with identical objects whereby little waiting is required, such as putting straws in a plastic bottle, can introduce waiting for another person to finish. Narrate intentions (e.g., "I am getting you your drink") and give visual cues when needed such as showing the child the cup or, if the child understands visual representations, a picture of a cup. Using a visual cue such as the sign for "wait" or a raised index finger to represent "1 minute" in conjunction with the word "wait" is also helpful over time. To help a child understand what "wait" means, use the word "waiting" in phrases such as "We are waiting our turn" for situations such as in the line at the grocery store while the child is happily eating a snack or in the drive-through while the child is happily playing with a toy. When the child is waiting appropriately, praise him or her, say-ing "Nice waiting while I get your _____." Once children can wait briefly, gradually increase the time between the child's request and the time when the child's request is granted. For example, when the child points to or says "cookie," at first wait a few seconds before hand-ing the cookie to him or her, and over time, gradually increase the wait by walking slowly to get the cookie, making a brief detour before giving the child the cookie and saying, "I have to get my cup and then I will give you a cookie." For a child who is working on following directions (see Chapter 6) or who is able to follow directions, teach replacement behaviors that are incompatible with the undesired behavior. For example, for a child who grabs, teach the child to follow directions such as "Hands down," "Fold your hands," or "Show me waiting hands." For a child who uses some words, count while getting requested items, saying "Let's count while I get your _____," and when counting is the routine, tell the child to count while you are getting what he or she wants. For a child who understands more complex language, tell the child, "I will _____ after _____" or "First _____, then _____." When children understand and comply with "First _____, then _____," regulation often improves. When teaching "first–then," it helps to begin with a direction in the child's repertoire or one that can easily be physically prompted *and* when the child exhibits motivation for an item or activity. For example, if a child requests a cookie nonverbally or verbally, tell the child "Sure, first high-five, then cookie." If the child does not give a high-five, take the child's hand to give the high-five and immediately give the child the cookie. Over time, prompt less until the child does not need assistance. This technique works well when used across a variety of routines in which the child exhibits motivation, such as when a child says or points "down" to get out of the booster seat after eating or when handing an item to an adult for help. When a child understands "first–then," he or she then will be ready for "one more, then done," which also assists with waiting.

Tips and Hints to Help Regain Regulation

When a young child is very upset and aggression such as throwing or hitting is likely, it is usually best to stay a few feet away rather than approach the child. If the child self-soothes using a pacifier, a blanket, or a pillow, it is helpful to have these items nearby so the child can get them. If one approaches the child who is in the midst of a tantrum, depending on the child, there is a chance the child may hit, kick, or throw an item that is being handed to him or her. When the item is nearby, it is up to the child to obtain it, which fosters independence and self-regulation. In addition, some children who are handed a pacifier, a blanket, or another favorite item when upset may later use screaming, hitting, kicking, or throwing as a way to request these preferred items.

Many times, young children bang their heads or hit themselves when frustrated. These behaviors are very scary for many parents. If a child bangs his or her head and is in danger of being hurt, he or she should be moved to a softer surface. In most cases, as long as children do not get what they wanted from doing so, these behaviors go away. It is very important, however, that support from someone specifically trained in eliminating severe challenging behaviors be obtained when self-injurious behaviors are present.

One technique that works well to diffuse a tantrum is ignoring the child and engaging in an activity he or she enjoys (e.g., putting items in a container or looking at a book) in close enough proximity that the child might be tempted to join when ready but far enough away so he or she will not immediately throw or hit. To do this, engage in the activity without looking at the child, because often if the child knows one is trying to interact, the child in the midst of a tantrum will become more dysregulated. When the child is calm and shows signs of interest, invite but do not require engagement (e.g., by offering an item to put in the container, by showing a picture from the book, by extending open arms for a hug). It is best to be positioned so the child must move a short distance. This enables the adult to anticipate (by observing body language and/or vocal or verbal communication such as screams or an emphatic "no") whether the offer will be accepted or rejected and try to avoid escalation of the tantrum. Often, at the end of a tantrum, cries of anger change to cries of sadness or cries that indicate "I need help." At that point, the aggression and screams are over and young children are much more likely to be calmed by being held.

A tantrum should *never* result in a child getting what he or she wanted that evoked the tantrum. If a child has tantrums to avoid something, he or she will learn that tantrums mean demands are stopped. If a child has tantrums and gets a desired item, he or she will learn to have a tantrum to get what he or she wants. When upset, however, children (and adults) often are unable to communicate as well as when they are calm and regulated, so any attempt to communicate appropriately, such as a gesture or a point, should be accepted, even if the child is verbal. If the child is not yet consistently using nonverbal communication such as eye gaze or a reach or point to communicate, or if the child is too upset to use his or her typical nonverbal or verbal communication methods, whenever possible, help the child use a gesture to indicate what is wanted. Another option is to wait for a momentary cease in screaming before presenting the desired item. If the child is crying or screaming to escape from a demand, if possible, gently physically assist the child to follow the direction. If this is not possible and one finds oneself in the position of "losing a battle," it is helpful to give the child a direction such as "Give me five," for which the child can be helped if the child does not or cannot follow the direction. When the child is calm and regulated, strategies to facilitate higher level skills on which the child is working should be used, but not when the child is dysregulated.

If undesirable behaviors decrease and desired behaviors increase, it is likely that the function of the behavior was targeted and replacement behaviors and skills are being addressed. When challenging behaviors do not improve, the team should consider an FBA (see Chapter 3).

In the following section, common routines and their regulatory challenges are presented. Their relevance to Making Sense of Self, Others, and the Environment; Flexibility; and Social Communication are discussed, followed by Tips and Hints specific to that routine. Because dysregulation is often related to skill deficits, strategies presented in the following chapters on Making Sense of Self, Others, and the Environment; Flexibility; and Social Communication will also assist with Regulation.

Bath Time

Common regulatory challenges at bath time include persistent splashing of water on the floor and dysregulation during washing, drying, and transitions in and/or out of the tub.

Making Sense of Self, Others, and the Environment: The child may not like the feel of the washcloth, the soap, the towel, the temperature of the water, or the water in his or her eyes; the sound of the water; the smell of the soap or shampoo; or the sight of the bubbles floating in the water.

Flexibility: The child may become upset if the bath time routine is different in terms of the sequence, who is present, or the items used.

Social Communication: The child may be unable to express his or her wants and needs related to staying in the tub, getting out of the tub, wanting a specific toy, wanting help with bathing, or wanting the washing or rinsing to stop.

Bedtime

In early childhood, young children typically spend more time asleep than awake. Sleep is needed for developmental processes and brain maturation, and sleep problems are the leading reason parents seek professional help (El-Sheikh & Sadeh, 2015). Parents report a variety of sleep problems in children diagnosed with autism, including difficulty falling asleep, more night awakenings, earlier awakenings, decreased amount of sleep, and more frequent walking and talking during sleep (Mayes, Calhoun, Bixler, & Vgontzas, 2009).

Making Sense of Self, Others, and the Environment: The child may not recognize signs of being tired, may not like the feel or smell of pajamas or the sheets, or may be confused by shadows on the wall or the movement of a curtain. The child may need a bedtime routine that signals it is time for bed.

Flexibility: The child may be upset if the sheets, blanket, or pajamas are different in terms of color, texture, or size, if someone else puts the child to bed, or if the books read or songs sung have changed.

Social Communication: The child may not be able to express wants and needs, such as the desire for a drink, for another person to tuck him or her in, or for a stuffed animal that is in another room.

Tips and Hints to Support Regulation at Bedtime

Many children try to delay bedtime, and children who are able to communicate often request one desire after another to stall the process. When parents find themselves in the situation in which turning off the light and saying goodnight results in a longer and longer list of requests such as "I need a drink," "I need one more kiss," and "I want Daddy to come kiss me," it is helpful to anticipate the previously used tactics and meet the needs, if appropriate, before walking out the door.

Setting limits regarding sleep is very challenging. When a child cries, runs around the house, or is otherwise dysregulated at bedtime or in the middle of the night, often parents sleep in the child's room, bring the child to their room, give the child something to eat or drink, rub the child's back, or turn on movies or television shows in order to get through the night. The challenges are often compounded by the sleep needs of others in the home, fear that neighbors may call the police, or concerns related to medical conditions or safety factors. When helping families with their children's sleeping difficulties, it is important to consider all the factors affecting the challenges. In the authors' experience, when toddlers do not readily adhere to limits and cooperate during daytime routines, it is unlikely they will follow directions and readily accept limits and denials at bedtime. Before expecting a child to follow bedtime rules, it is often necessary for providers to help families learn to gain cooperation and compliance with tasks such as helping to clean up toys, coming when called, holding hands when taking a walk, and placing a cup rather than throwing it when finished drinking. Once a child is able to follow a variety of directions and participate in a variety of routines, he or she will be more likely to cooperate and accept limits and denials at bedtime.

Book Time

Many young children with autism and related disorders enjoy looking at books but become dysregulated when others "interfere" with the activity.

Making Sense of Self, Others, and the Environment: The child may not like a sensory property of the book such as the look of certain pictures, the feel of some textured pages, or the topic of the book. The child may want to get tactile or visual stimulation from the book itself and may want to hold it.

Flexibility: The child may want the book to be read a certain way or by a certain person because that is what usually occurs. The child may only want to look at certain books, may want to hold the book upside down, or may want to control the book and may have a tantrum when others hold it.

Social Communication: The child may be unable to communicate the desire for a different book or the desire to look at the book independently.

Tips and Hints to Support Regulation at Book Time

For children who look at books independently but who become dysregulated when others read to them, begin talking briefly about familiar pictures on each page. If the child shows little interest, begin with one or two pages and gradually increase the adult direction. Use "One more, then done" when reading the second to last page that will be read.

For children who show little or no interest in books and become dysregulated during book time, make a book using a small photo album and use photos of favorite people and pictures of preferred items such as favorite toys, foods, or stuffed animals.

For children who resist when others read to them, begin by labeling or interjecting comments about one or two pictures that may be of interest to the child. Gradually increase the number of comments as the interaction is tolerated. Some children dislike when others hold books, but they often will relinquish the control as they begin to tolerate this type of interaction. Once children stay regulated when others hold the books and name items, they are ready for directions to touch a picture of a familiar object or person or character. Using books that have the same object, character, or person on many of the pages affords opportunities for practice and repetition.

Community Outings

Community outings can be very stressful for young children with ASD and for their families and caregivers.

Making Sense of Self, Others, and the Environment: The child may not know where he or she is going; the child may not like to be confined in the car seat, the grocery cart, or the stroller; the child may not like the smells of the destination; and/or the child may not be familiar with a sound and/or its source; or the child may feel uncomfortable with movement.

Flexibility: The child may be upset if the route changes, if the sequence of events differs, or if the schedule changes and the outing is not a typical part of the day.

Social Communication: The child may be unable to communicate wants and needs due to unfamiliarity of the environment.

Tips and Hints to Support Regulation During Community Outings

Many children with ASD become dysregulated when they must follow safety rules such as holding hands or walking next to an adult. A strategy that works well is telling the child "Hold my hand or you will go in the stroller." As soon as the child lets go of the adult's hand, the adult puts the child in the stroller for several minutes. At the end of that time, the child is taken out of the stroller and again told "Hold my hand or you will go in the stroller." The child is praised for holding the adult's hand and, as soon as the child lets go, he or she is put back in the stroller. Some children learn this quickly, whereas others need to practice multiple times in multiple settings.

Many parents give their child a snack while the child sits in the grocery cart. This strategy can be effective as long as the snack is given when the child is behaving appropriately rather than after the child begins to demonstrate unwanted behaviors; in the latter case, the child will learn that dysregulation results in a snack.

Diapering and Dressing/Grooming and Hygiene

Many children become dysregulated during diapering and dressing and grooming and hygiene. Changing diapers, going to the bathroom, getting dressed and undressed, brushing teeth, brushing and combing hair, and washing hands and face often disrupt activities that are more fun.

Making Sense of Self, Others, and the Environment: The child may not like the feeling of the diaper, the wipes, the clothing, the toothbrush, the washcloth, or other materials involved in the routine, and the routine, from the child's point of view, may be unnecessary.

Flexibility: The child may want to wear the same clothing items every day or may feel that it is only a specific person's role to change the child's clothes or diapers and may become upset when the routine changes.

Social Communication: The child may not be able to express preferences for certain articles of clothing, certain people performing certain roles, or other desires.

Tips and Hints for Supporting Regulation During Diapering, Dressing, Grooming, and Hygiene Routines

Have a bag of small, washable toys and objects with which the child can choose to play during diaper changes. Rotate the bag's contents so the child will not tire of them. Give the child the items before he or she begins to fuss and cry.

Be silly and playful to help the activity be as much fun as possible. For example, sing songs such as "This is the way we put on your pants," or play Peekaboo when putting a shirt over the child's face or "This Little Piggy" when putting on socks.

Have the child help as much as possible to increase not only cooperation but also independence in self-care.

If the child frequently has tantrums during dressing and diapering, try changing him or her in a different position or in a different place. In addition, try diapering and dressing while he or she is watching television or a movie. If the child is calm, do this for a few days to break the routine of the dysregulation and then reintroduce the routine without the distraction.

Household Activities

Some children become dysregulated when parents are busy with cooking, cleaning, or tending to other children and/or when they are required to participate in household activities.

Making Sense of Self, Others, and the Environment: The child may not want to do a household activity because it is not meaningful to the child. He or she may not like when the parent's attention is directed away from him or her. The child may not like the smell of household cleaners or the sound of appliances such as the vacuum or the mixer.

Flexibility: The child may be upset if the household activity does not fit with the child's plan or if it occurs at a different time, in a different place, or with different people than usual.

Social Communication: The child may be unable to communicate a desire to help, a desire not to help, or the desire to do a household activity in a different way or at a different time.

Tips and Hints to Support Regulation During Household Activities

When a child has difficulty finding appropriate things to do when parents are busy, it is tempting for parents to refrain from interacting with the child out of fear that talking to the child will result in the child being clingy or demanding attention in other ways. At times, however, if attention is given intermittently when a parent is busy with a household activity, the child will continue to play, and inappropriate attention-getting behavior such as screaming, crying, or "looking for trouble" can be avoided.

Mealtime/Snack Time

Mealtime and snack time can be very stressful for many children and families during preparation, during the meal itself, or during cleanup.

Making Sense of Self, Others, and the Environment: The child may not recognize signs of hunger or thirst; may not like the feel of the bib; may not like the look, smell, or taste of the food; or may not like being confined in a highchair or booster seat.

Flexibility: The child may be upset if the food, plates, cups, and/or utensils are different; if the eating schedule has changed; if the person preparing or feeding him or her is different; if the bib is different; or if someone put an unwanted food item in front of him or her.

Social Communication: The child may be unable to communicate the desire for or a dislike of a certain food; the desire for food to be cut in a certain shape or size; the desire to be fed; the desire to self-feed; the desire to be done with mealtime; or the desire for different cups, plates, or utensils.

Tips and Hints to Support Regulation During Mealtime/Snack Time

For a child who becomes dysregulated when put in the highchair or booster seat and who does not stay at the table long enough to eat a sufficient amount, use the highchair or booster seat for preferred activities such as playing with modeling dough, coloring, watching a movie, or playing an app on a tablet. Introduce food during or at the end of these activities so that eating eventually becomes associated with sitting in the highchair or booster seat.

Playtime

Dysregulation during playtime can be caused by the play activity itself or by interactions with others during play. Some children with ASD are quite self-directed in their play and it is very difficult to join them. When approached, some children immediately walk away and others have a tantrum.

Making Sense of Self, Others, and the Environment: Dysregulation can occur under a variety of conditions, including when a child cannot predict that blocks fall, when an electronic toy needs new batteries, or when the sensory properties of toys and materials are interpreted as unpleasant or confusing.

Flexibility: The child may have a tantrum if someone disturbs the figures he or she put in a line, if someone else is playing with a toy he or she thinks is his or hers, or if a person does not play in the way the child anticipates, which changes the play routine.

Social Communication: The child may become upset if he or she cannot communicate what, where, or how he or she wants to play with toys, materials, or others.

Tips and Hints to Support Regulation During Playtime

For children who dysregulate when others approach them when they are playing, it is helpful to hand them items they need during their play activity to begin to establish rapport. For example, if a child is lining up blocks, the other person can hand him or her blocks to add to the line. The other person can join the child's play in this manner until the child views the person as a helper rather than a menace.

Being playful and silly is a good way to help a child develop trust and regulation during play. For example, putting a cloth or a soft toy on one's head and pretending to sneeze—causing the item to fall to the floor—often brings smiles to a child who may be fearful or self-absorbed.

Tips for Monitoring Progress in Regulation

Progress in Regulation can be monitored using the following:

A parent rating scale of the child's cooperation during routines

A list of ways the child calmed himself or herself

A list of new routines in which the child participated without dysregulation

A list of routines in which the child waited, asked for help, or communicated wants and needs in appropriate ways rather than by screaming

A record of the number of times the child exhibited specific behaviors, such as hitting, throwing, or biting during specific routines

A record of the length of time the child participated in a specific activity without exhibiting specified behaviors such as screaming, hitting, or running away

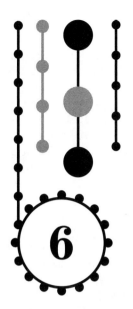

6

Building Skills to Support Making Sense of Self, Others, and the Environment

Infants and toddlers learn about themselves, others, and the environment as they integrate skills across all domains of development. After taking in information via their sensory systems, they respond in a variety of ways that depend upon their states of regulation and arousal, their temperaments and personalities, their previous experiences, the intensities of the sensations, their likes or dislikes of the sensations, other happenings in the environment, and their repertoires of skills. For example, when the smoke detector emitted its alarm due to crumbs burning in the toaster, each of the five children in a private child care setting reacted differently. Mary, who was not yet mobile, covered her head with her blanket, covered her ears, and cried; Johnny crawled into the kitchen to look for the source of the sound; Maritza ran to the door and asked, "What's that?"; Alexander crawled to find the babysitter; and Hakim jumped up and down, smiling.

In the early years, children participate in reciprocal interactions with others and with the environment, which results in forming expectations about objects, events, others, and themselves (Wang & Barrett, 2012). These reciprocal interactions involve a myriad of skills related to attending and responding. Children learn about information from all of their senses: visual, auditory, tactile, gustatory (taste), olfactory (smell), vestibular (balance/movement), and proprioceptive (body position), and they learn to focus on certain sensations and to tune out others. This selective attention contributes to social, cognitive, linguistic, and perceptual development (Bahrick & Lickliter, 2014).

The concept of self, according to cognitive neuroscience literature, involves knowing that one is the cause of one's actions and thoughts and knowing that one is distinct from others and from the environment. Self-recognition and body awareness are components of self-awareness (Lyons & Fitzgerald, 2013). Self-awareness is thought to be related to understanding of others' emotional states, a component of theory of mind, a term first used by Premack and Woodruff (1978) that refers to one's ability to impute mental states to others as well as oneself. Theory of mind is necessary for sympathy, empathy, and perspective taking. In their review of the literature, Lyons and Fitzgerald highlighted many processes related to self–other awareness, including gaze following, responses to sounds, attention, showing to others, responding to name, looking at faces, pretend play, and pointing. There are many theories about how these developmental processes occur in children who are progressing typically and even more regarding children who present with symptoms of autism and related disorders. The word *autism* is derived from the Greek word meaning *self,* and many researchers, including Kanner

(1943), describe atypical self-concept development in autism. This topic can be found not only in early writings about autism but also in more recent works (Duff & Flattery, 2014; Lyons & Fitzgerald).

Sensory processing in individuals with ASD is another topic that is fraught with many theories and opinions due to inconsistencies in terminology across disciplines (Baranek et al., 2014; Schaaf & Lane, 2014). In their review of research using a standardized rating scale of sensory symptoms, Hazen, Stornelli, O'Rourke, Koesterer, and McDougle (2014) found prevalence estimates varying from 69% to 95% of individuals with ASD who showed a high frequency of sensory symptoms. They noted that the broad range reflected differences in methodology and populations. In their review of the literature, Schaaf and Lane (2014) cited prevalence rates ranging from 45% to 96% of reported sensory features in autism.

Sensory features in autism have been categorized in a variety of ways. Baranek et al. (2014) cited four sensory patterns but said others may exist. The four patterns they cited are 1) hyporesponsive or underreactive to sensory input (e.g., less than typical pain awareness, excessive spinning without showing signs of dizziness, lack of orienting to sounds); 2) hyperresponsive or overreactive to sensory input (e.g., covering ears in response to sounds, avoidance of textures of clothing or sticky substances typically tolerated by others); 3) sensory interests, repetitions, and seeking behaviors (e.g., preoccupations with fans, lining up toys, excessive jumping); and 4) enhanced perception (e.g., alerting to sounds others do not readily perceive). Schaaf and Lane (2014), in their review of the literature, grouped sensory features into three categories: sensory reactivity and unusual interests, sensory perception, and sensory integration. One of these, sensory integration, is laden with controversy. Often the term refers to a theory developed by Ayres (1972), and advocates and critics argue as to its effectiveness. Ayres (1979) defined sensory integration as "the organization of sensory information for use" (p. 1), and the theory proposes that sensory input must be actively organized and used to act upon the environment in order for optimal learning, behavior, and participation to occur. Atypical perception of sensory information or atypical organization of the information can lead to challenges in learning, behavior, and/or participation.

Because of a lack of consistency in use, the term *Ayres Sensory Integration* is now trademarked and encompasses Ayres' theory and methods of assessment and treatment (Parham & Mailloux, 2015). The lack of consistency in use of the term, the procedures used, and its efficacy has contributed to the controversy (Parham et al., 2007). In addition, there has been criticism of the methodology in many of the studies of sensory integration (Ashburner, Rodger, Ziviani, & Hinder, 2014; Lang et al., 2012). Case-Smith, Weaver, and Fristad (2014) differentiated between sensory integration therapy and sensory-based interventions, as these are often confused in the literature. Sensory integration therapy is based on Ayres' theory and occurs in a clinic. It consists of play-based activities that provide challenges that are not too difficult and not too easy and require using sensory information to respond adaptively. For example, a young child may swing in a hammock and throw balls of different sizes and weights into baskets placed around the swing, necessitating integration of a variety of sensations. Sensory-based strategies, on the other hand, are adult-directed strategies that are integrated into a child's daily routine to improve behavior regulation (e.g., massaging or rocking to calm a child). Though there is controversy regarding the term sensory integration when it refers to the therapeutic modality, research suggests that many individuals with autism have difficulties integrating sensory information (Barenek et al., 2014; Marco, Hinkley, Hill, & Nagarajan, 2011).

The majority of the research on sensory features in ASD has focused on sensory over-responsivity (SOR), which is also referred to as hypersensitivity or hyperresponsivity.

SOR is characterized by atypically intense and prolonged negative reactions to sensory stimuli that often are manifested by anxiety, tantrums, distractibility, avoidance and escape behaviors, and aggression. SOR in toddlers, as well as in older children who have ASD, has been associated with increased maternal stress and increased restriction of family activities (Ben-Sasson, Soto, Martínez-Pedraza, & Carter, 2013). Green et al. (2013) found evidence using neuroimaging that individuals with ASD showed greater activation in multiple parts of their brains in response to mildly aversive sensory stimuli compared with individuals who were typically developing. These responses were located in areas of the brain related to sensory processing, regulation, and emotion processing. Sometimes, individuals with ASD appear to be hyporesponsive to sensory input when they are engaging in sensory seeking behaviors (Patten, Ausderau, Watson, & Baranek, 2013). For example, a young child who is intently watching a ceiling fan may not shift attention and orient to environmental sounds or voices. In addition, some children show a decreased response to pain when they are seeking movement and deep pressure such as when jumping and landing on their knees.

Restrictive and repetitive behaviors often involve sensory seeking, such as when a child twirls or spins objects, throws items onto a hard surface to watch and hear the results, or squeezes into tight spaces. In the authors' experiences, at times children perform these behaviors because they are fun and feel good and at other times because the children do not know what else to do. A child may demonstrate the same behavior for different reasons, all of which must be determined in order to effectively change the behavior. As discussed in Chapter 3, in order to change behavior it is necessary to determine its function, and this applies to behaviors that involve the sensory system. When a teething toddler bites due to discomfort, a teether is likely to help; however, when a toddler bites to obtain a toy, a teether likely will not be a useful substitute for the wanted toy.

Behaviors may be due to sensory seeking or automatic reinforcement, but they also may be to escape, avoid, or gain something. Collin may rock vigorously on the couch for a variety of reasons; for example, 1) he enjoys the vestibular, visual, auditory, and/or proprioceptive sensations, 2) he does not have anything else to do, either due to a skill deficit or to a lack of motivation, or 3) in the past, his aunt, who was worried that he would hurt himself, gave him a cookie to eat, which stopped his rocking and taught him that rocking was a way to request a cookie.

Sensation avoiding must also be looked at from the perspective of the function and what else is happening in the environment. Kimberly screamed every time her mother washed her hands, and her mother thought it was due to the feeling of the water and the soap on her hand. Her mother tried different soaps and different temperatures of the water—as she had done with Kimberly's older brother, who preferred cool water and bar soap rather than liquid soap—but still Kimberly screamed. Her EI provider suggested water play with soap, and Kimberly happily played during the activity. Kimberly's EI provider asked to see the hand washing routine and observed that Kimberly became agitated as soon as her mother turned on the light. The EI provider asked her mother to turn off the light and then noticed that Kimberly was reaching for the light switch. The provider asked Kimberly's mother to hold her up to the light switch and ask her if she wanted to turn on the light. Kimberly did so and washed her hands without screaming. Many individuals with autism exhibit sensory differences and challenging behaviors, and sometimes the challenging behaviors are due to the sensory differences, but not always. Observation and testing of hypotheses are necessary to determine causes of sensory seeking and sensory avoiding behaviors.

Often children with ASD do not readily interact with toys or materials in functional ways. This may be due to a lack of motivation to use the toys or objects. Sometimes, this lack of motivation is due to a skill deficit related to motor processing. Atypical motor skills have been found to be a feature of ASD. In their review of the literature, Fabbri-Destro, Gizzonio, and Avanzini (2013) discussed atypical motor features including clumsiness, poor postural stability, atypical gait, decreased anticipation and planning (including delayed or absent protective responses and delayed prepositioning of the hand based on the size and shape of an object), and challenges with imitation and motor planning.

Motor planning and praxis also fit into the category of confusing and complicated terms with definitions and usage that vary within and across disciplines. In 1995, Dewey wrote about this variability, and a consensus has not emerged thus far in the literature. In this book, *motor planning/praxis* is defined as the ability to formulate an idea and perform a series of steps to accomplish a goal (Ayres, 1985). Those who exhibit motor planning challenges may have challenges at any part of the process, which may manifest as a lack of ideas, a lack of plans, or a lack of efficiency in carrying out the plan. Motor planning depends upon sensory processing, as one integrates information from the senses to perform motor responses. For example, to successfully navigate when walking in the woods, one must process visual, auditory, and proprioceptive information to maneuver over rocks and logs and search for the source of an approaching sound such as a runner or an animal. Once executing the steps becomes part of an individual's repertoire, planning is no longer required. For example, when first learning to drive a car, most people plan and sequence each step, but once driving has been practiced, most experienced drivers execute the steps with little thought. In young children, this can also be seen in motor sequences such as dressing and completing shape sorters and puzzles. Once practiced, much less conscious thought is needed to accomplish the goal. In their summary of the literature regarding children with praxis, motor planning, and motor coordination challenges, Lane, Ivey, and May-Benson (2014) described youngsters who had difficulties related to self-care, generalizing motor skills from one situation to another, generating ideas for actions, using tools, following visual or verbal directions, and interacting with novel items. According to Cossu et al. (2012), children with ASD frequently have motor difficulties, including challenges with imitation and challenges with recognition of other's motor intentions. These challenges affect motor planning as well as understanding of the goals of actions of others.

The term *affordance* refers to the match between a person and the environment that enables a particular action to be possible (Gibson, 1979; Ishak, Franchak, & Adolph, 2014). According to Linkenauger, Lerner, Ramenzoni, and Proffitt (2012), affordance perception is related to perceptual-motor integration. Perceptual-motor integration is related to processing sensory information and using it to make motor responses. This skill is used in everyday interactions including social interactions and the ability to predict the actions of others. Linkenauger et al. theorized that difficulties with affordance perception may account for the motor problems and the social communication challenges seen in individuals with ASD. Individuals with autism have been noted to have challenges predicting the actions of others; however, as is common in much of the literature on ASD, there are conflicting opinions (Berger & Ingersoll, 2014; Sparaci, Stefanini, D'Elia, Vicari, & Rizzolatti, 2014). As children develop, they learn to anticipate and predict after practice. The game of Peekaboo illustrates this concept well. Peekaboo evolves from a game whereby the adult initially plays the initiator and the responder while the infant demonstrates behaviors such as looking at himself or items in the environment unrelated to the game. This changes after practice, and the infant begins to make sense of the game as the adult persists: the infant changes the adult's behavior as the adult changes the volume or pitch of his or her voice, the timing of the interaction, and other features to capture the infant's attention (Tronick, 2013). This process appears to take much longer in young children who have ASD or red flags for being on the spectrum. As one of the authors stated to the other when writing this book, "Many of the children I work with don't understand Peekaboo for a very long time."

Difficulties understanding others' intentions in individuals who have ASD and related disorders have been associated with difficulties with attention (Shic, Bradshaw, Klin, Scassellati, & Chawarska, 2011) as well as difficulties with motor imitation (Vanvuchelen, Van Schuerbeeck, Roeyers, & De Weerdt, 2013). Imitation, a skill critical to learning and social acceptance, is another term with little consensus regarding its definition (Nadel, 2014). In her book *How Imitation Boosts Development in Infancy and Autism Spectrum Disorder*, Nadel discussed many important factors about the importance of examining what is being imitated and the timing of the imitation. What is being imitated depends upon one's motor repertoire, as it is impossible to imitate actions that are not in that repertoire. In addition, one must consider if the action is new to the individual, if the process or the end goal is being imitated rather than the actions themselves, and if knowledge about the items used is a cue that evokes the behavior as opposed to it being an imitative behavior. The timing of the imitation also is an important consideration. Imitation has a social communicative component when it is either immediate or delayed by a short amount of time but not when it is deferred, which occurs when the model is no longer present. Another crucial distinction regarding the timing of imitation is whether it is spontaneous or directed. Those who work in EI frequently see young children with ASD who use objects such as cups, brushes, combs, hammers, and push-button toys appropriately, yet when presented with a model of these actions and told "You do" or "Your turn," the children do not demonstrate the use of the object. One must then determine why imitation did not occur. For example, was there a lack of understanding of the expectation due to a receptive language problem, a lack of attention to the model, a lack of compliance to following directions, a motor planning problem that occurred under a demand situation, and/or a lack of motivation?

As discussed in Chapter 3, motivation is a key component to learning. Klintwall, Macari, Eikeseth, and Chawarska (2014) found that in toddlers with ASD, interest in toys, activities, and social routines were predictors of their rate of skill acquisition. A young child's participation in these routines and activities is dependent on his or her ability to Make Sense of Self, Others, and the Environment, and acquiring skills in these areas scaffolds further development in the same areas. EI providers coaching parents and caregivers to foster Making Sense of Self, Others, and the Environment should target the following skills: attends to sensory stimuli, tolerates sensory stimuli, shifts attention, imitates actions, and follows directions.

Attends to Sensory Stimuli

Background Information: Daily routines contain a variety of sensory information. Infants demonstrate attention to stimuli via alerting responses. In regard to vision, they look at and track objects and people and squint in bright lights. They show eye-widening and turning to environmental sounds and voices. In the area of touch, infants feel items that are touched to their hands or that they grasp, suck when they feel the nipple on their lips, and move away from unpleasant items such as nasal aspirators. When bounced and rocked, they may smile or calm or move to indicate that they want more.

Relevance to Children with Autism: In young children with autism, it is often difficult to distinguish hyposensitivity from difficulties shifting attention, as both may result in a lack of attention to sensory stimuli. In their review of the literature, Patten et al. (2013) found sensory hyporesponsivity to be inversely associated with language development in children with ASD. Preferential visual attention to motion as well as preferential attention to others' eyes are seen in infants and toddlers who are developing typically but are lacking in infants and toddlers who have ASD (Klin, Shultz, & Jones, 2015). Research regarding auditory responses in children with ASD has revealed enhanced pitch perception and reduced orientation to sounds (O'Connor, 2012).

How to Incorporate into Routines: Note that not all activities are appropriate for all children or families, and some adaptations may be needed to assist children to participate if they are not yet attending to a variety of sensory experiences.

Bath Time

Auditory: Talk about the bath time process, highlighting what is being washed, the temperature of the water, the toys being played with, and other relevant topics. Sing a song such as "This Is the Way We Wash Your ____." Make silly noises when washing and drying the child.

Olfactory: Provide a variety of scented shampoos, body washes, and soaps.

Tactile and Proprioceptive: Use a variety of textures of washcloths and towels, and vary the pressure when washing and drying the child. Massage the child after the bath.

Visual: Vary the environment by providing different tub toys. At times, use bubble bath or tablets that change the color of the water or blow bubbles.

Bedtime

Auditory: Sing favorite songs and talk about events of the day and bedtime routine.

Olfactory: Place essential oils or other scented items in the room, out of the child's reach for safety.

Tactile and Proprioceptive: Massage the child with relaxing scented oils and soft cloths. Cuddle, pat, and caress the child as he or she relaxes.

Vestibular: Rock the child for a few minutes before putting him or her in the bed or crib.

Visual: Shine a flashlight in the darkened room. Use light bulbs or lenses of differing colors.

Book Time

Auditory: Choose books that have pictures that go with environmental sounds that can be modeled, such as doors upon which to "knock-knock," cars that "beep-beep," and animals that make their sounds.

Olfactory: Provide scratch-and-sniff books or make your own using scented stickers.

Tactile: Provide books with a variety of textures to feel.

Proprioceptive: Choose books that have moving parts for the child to manipulate.

Vestibular: Choose books with actions such as jumping, rowing a boat, or doing flips, and engage the child in the action of the story.

Visual: Consider how visually "busy" the book is. If a child is not yet attending well to pictures, choose books with patterns, progress to ones that have one or two pictures per page, and then choose ones that have more pictures per page as the child's visual attention improves. Make a book of pictures or photos of familiar objects and people using a small photo album.

Community Outings

Auditory: Provide opportunities for the child to hear birds singing, vehicles honking, sirens blaring, train whistles blowing, rain falling, thunder clapping, people singing, different types of music playing, lawn mowers whirring, snow blowers churning, leaf blowers bellowing, and other environmental sounds.

Gustatory: Taste new foods from a salad bar, a frozen yogurt or ice cream shop, or a bakery.

Olfactory: Expose the child to the perfume counter in department stores, bakeries, candy stores, marshmallows toasting on a campfire, freshly mown grass, and farms.

Tactile and Visual: Help or have the child pick fruits and vegetables, play in the sand at the park or beach, walk barefoot in the grass, and gather stones, leaves, and sticks.

Proprioceptive: Help or have the child jump over the cracks in the sidewalk or from the bottom step of the slide, and wrap up and snuggle in a towel or blanket at the beach.

Vestibular: Swing and slide at the park, participate in a semistructured movement class, go on rides at the amusement park or coin rides at the mall, ride a pony, maneuver a ride-on toy or tricycle, operate a single-switch electric powered toy vehicle, go the mall, and go for a ride in a wagon, stroller, or bicycle seat.

Visual: Go for car or stroller rides in the dark to look at lights, to a pet store or aquarium to watch fish swimming, to a train or bus station or construction site to watch vehicles, or to the mall to watch people on the escalator.

Diapering and Dressing

Auditory: Sing while diapering and dressing.

Olfactory: Before using a baby wipe or ointment, place it below the child's nose so he or she can smell the fragrance.

Tactile: Provide a variety of types of materials in clothing such as fleece, denim, corduroy, and cotton. Rub lotion on the child before dressing him or her. Playfully blow on his or her belly after a diaper change.

Proprioceptive: Give the child a massage before dressing, and playfully and gently shake his or her arms and legs.

Vestibular: Playfully and gently roll the child after dressing and diapering.

Visual: Play Peekaboo with a clean diaper or when pulling the shirt over the child's head.

Grooming and Hygiene

Auditory: Sing songs while washing and brushing teeth.

Gustatory: Use a variety of flavors of children's toothpaste.

Olfactory: Provide a variety of scents of soaps.

Tactile: Expose the child to a variety of textures of washcloths and towels. Before or after hand washing, rinse the child's hands in warm and cool water. Brush the child's teeth with a battery-operated toothbrush.

Visual: Perform grooming activities such as toothbrushing, hair brushing, and face washing in front of the mirror.

Household Activities

Auditory: Have the child help when using safe appliances that emit sounds, such as turning the vacuum cleaner on and off.

Proprioceptive: Have the child help carry "heavy" loads, such as the watering can and groceries, as well as push the vacuum and move the garbage cans to the curb.

Tactile: When doing yard work, give opportunities to dig in the dirt, place leaves in bags or bins, and play in the water when watering flowers or vegetable plants. Inside the home, the child can help wipe spills with a variety of textures of cloth and take clothes out of the washer and dryer to experience wet and warm fabric.

Vestibular: Provide opportunities for the child to roll down couch cushions that are removed to be vacuumed or roll down a hill when outdoors doing yard work.

Visual: When entering or leaving a room, have the child use the light switch.

Mealtime/Snack Time

Auditory: Allow the child to turn the food processor or blender on and off. Have the child push the start button on the microwave to hear it start and beep when it stops. Count down with the timer on the microwave.

Gustatory and Olfactory: Allow the child to taste and smell appropriate foods during cooking and food preparation.

Tactile and Proprioceptive: Have the child place vegetables in the bowl and/or tear lettuce to help make a salad, peel a banana, open packages of food, and pour liquids.

Visual: Show the child liquids being poured or mixed and the time counting down on the microwave.

Playtime

Auditory: Expose the child to music, humming, singing, whistling, and silly sounds. Provide pots, pans, and large spoons to bang, musical toys to activate, and plastic bottles with secured lids filled with uncooked rice, beans, or coins to shake.

Gustatory and Olfactory: Have a tea party with a variety of foods and drinks.

Proprioceptive: Incorporate activities such as banging on pots and pans or drums when singing songs. Give opportunities to jump on pillows or off a low stool. Give playful squeezes, singing "This Is the Way We Squeeze Your _____" and naming the body part being squeezed. Gently wrap the child in a small blanket or towel, keeping his or head uncovered to watch for signs of distress as well as to ensure the airway is not blocked, and playfully squeeze. Give the child modeling dough to squeeze or poke.

Tactile: Be playful with stuffed animals and clothing of varied textures when tickling, patting, or massaging a child. Make an indoor "sand box" using a bin or box of dried pasta, dried beans, or uncooked rice. If the child puts inedible objects in his or her mouth, use dried cereal instead. Provide finger paints or, for children who put inedible items in their mouths and/or who would also benefit from tasting or smelling food, use whipped cream, whipped topping, ketchup, mustard, or pudding.

Vestibular: Incorporate movement into play by gently rocking, swinging, bouncing, rolling, flipping, and dancing. When two adults are present, swing the child in a strong blanket.

Tips and Hints for Attending to Sensory Stimuli

For each sensory system, assess to which type of stimuli the child attends best. For example, with visual stimuli, does the child alert more to certain colors, patterns, or movement of the visual stimuli; with auditory stimuli, does the child turn more to singing, higher-pitched voices, lower-pitched voices, or fluctuating intonation; and with vestibular/proprioceptive stimuli, does the child show positive responses and alerting to gentle bouncing or rougher irregular movements?

Concentrate on one or two sensations at a time rather than inundate the child with a lot of sensory information at once.

Observe the child's emotional and motor responses to determine whether the stimulation is pleasantly alerting, the goal for gaining attention.

If the child tends to get overstimulated or upset, use the process of elimination to assess what sensory modality or modalities are affecting the ability to attend.

If the child tends to be overly focused on a certain stimulus that is not being targeted, eliminate the source so the child is better able to focus on the sensory response being targeted. For example, if the child is visually stimming on a fan and not attending to a song, a book, a massage, or the person who is interacting, turn off the fan or turn the child so he or she is not facing the distraction and can focus on the desired stimulus.

Ideas for Monitoring Progress: Note new types of sensation to which the child shows a response, such as smiling, turning toward, or moving to show a desire for more.

Tolerates Sensory Stimuli

Background Information: Once a child alerts to or processes a sensory stimulus, he or she responds in a positive, negative, or neutral manner. Negative responses can interfere with a child's participation in daily routines and activities.

Relevance to Children with Autism: In their review of the literature, Ben-Sasson et al. (2013) found that 56%–79% of children with autism have SOR. These responses can greatly affect the child and the family in terms of participation in routines. SOR can occur in one sensory system alone or in multiple sensory systems and can vary from one moment to another, making it difficult to discern the strategies needed to help the child in a given situation and across time. Often a child may react to one specific aspect within a sensory system. For example, a child may enjoy movement in a particular plane such as bouncing up and down but may become upset if flipped upside down. Similarly, a child may enjoy moving in a variety of ways, but if someone imposes the same type of movements on him or her, the child may become upset. At times it is challenging to figure out what sensation the child is reacting to and under what conditions. For example, during messy activities in his classroom (e.g., finger painting, pulling seeds from the pumpkin at Halloween), when the teacher took his hand to help him participate, Jebediah screamed and left the table. At mealtime, however, whenever he had ketchup, applesauce, or pudding on his plate, Jebediah rubbed the food into his hands and face and giggled. Only after a great deal of assessment, watching Jebediah in a variety of activities and initiating many discussions with his family and teachers, was his EI provider able to discern what Jebediah was reacting to in order to give strategies to increase his participation in messy activities. His refusals to participate and his often subsequent outbursts were related not only to tactile stimuli but also to challenges with flexibility and understanding other's intentions.

How to Incorporate into Routines: Note that sensory activities should always begin where the child is comfortable; gradually increase the duration and intensity of the sensation to help the child adapt. It is important to prioritize which sensations should be addressed and during which routines so the child and the parents are not stressed from working on too much at once.

Bath Time

Auditory: If the child reacts negatively to the sound of the running water, first try having a slow, gentle stream of water and, over time, gradually increase the amount of force as the child adapts. Have the child turn the water on and off when outside of the tub so he or she can control the sensory input.

Olfactory: Try different soaps and shampoos to determine any preferences, and once preferences have been found, gradually introduce new scents.

Tactile: If a child dislikes water in his or her face, during hair rinsing, hold a washcloth over the child's eyes or place a sticker or picture of a favorite character on the ceiling for the child to look at, which will tilt the head in a position to decrease the water flow over the face. If the child dislikes being washed, use cues such as "Time to wash your _____," pointing or touching the body part to help prepare the child. Determine if lighter or firmer touch is better tolerated. If the child is able, have him or her help wash. Over time, decrease accommodations to help the child gain new acceptance.

Vestibular: If the child does not like being tipped backward, use a bowl to rinse the hair while the child is in a sitting position.

Visual: For children who do not like bubbles in the water or changes to the color of the water when bubble bath or color-changing tablets are used, first use small amounts and gradually increase as tolerance improves. Allow the child to choose the color of the soap, tablets, bubbles, or other medium that is not readily accepted.

Bedtime

SOR has been correlated with difficulties going to sleep and staying asleep (Mazurek & Petroski, 2015). To help a child fall asleep, it is important that the environment be calming. For children who tend to be overly sensitive, one must carefully assess the environment and, when possible, modify sensory stimuli to encourage sleep. For children who are poor sleepers and very sensitive, strategies to increases tolerance at bedtime must be implemented very carefully to ensure that bedtime stress is not too great for the child and the parents.

Auditory: Dampen or eliminate sounds that interfere with falling or staying asleep. Over time, gradually increase sounds so the child becomes accustomed to sleeping in noisier environments.

Tactile: For children who do not tolerate the feeling of specific pajamas, blankets, or sheets, accommodate their preferences. Then, over time, if sleeping patterns are well established, gradually introduce fabrics that feel similar. When the new texture is tolerated, introduce another new but similar feeling material.

Visual: Limit visual distractions such as toys, lights, light switches, or pictures that may interfere with relaxation and sleep. Choose books for the bedtime story that have pictures that are not overly exciting. Consider furniture placement to reduce visual distractions. Over time, gradually introduce more distractions as tolerated.

Book Time

If book time is an enjoyed routine, it can be used as a time to expose the child to sensations that are not well tolerated, as the child may be distracted and more tolerant.

Auditory: If the child does not like certain sounds that can be replicated, playfully and briefly incorporate them when appropriate into a favorite book. As the child tolerates the sound, gradually increase the volume or the duration.

Olfactory: Provide scratch-and-sniff books or make your own using scented stickers to expand the child's acceptance of new smells.

Tactile: Provide books with different textures for the child to feel and explore. If certain textures of fabric are avoided, make a book using pictures of favorite objects from the problematic fabrics. For children who resist being confined in a car seat or highchair, reading a favorite book while sitting in the seat may help desensitize them.

Vestibular: Children who avoid rocking in a rocking chair or swinging on a swing may be willing to sit on an adult's lap in a rocking chair or on a swing to look at books. At first the chair or swing may need to be still, but as the children become interested in the books, they may be able to tolerate slow, gentle excursions of movement.

Visual: Some parents of children with ASD have reported their children do not like specific pictures, such as those of farm animals. Provide books that have only a few such pictures and gradually increase the child's exposure over time.

Community Outings

Auditory: Try to anticipate sounds that the child may not anticipate or may not understand. For example, when stopped at a railroad crossing before the train appears, tell the child, "Here comes the train. Get ready to hear 'choo-choo.'"

Gustatory: Some children more readily taste new foods when in a restaurant or when they are allowed to choose foods at a buffet or salad bar than when they are at home. Place only a small amount of a new food on the child's plate so it does not seem overwhelming.

Olfactory: If a child reacts to a scent or odor that is identifiable, label it and draw the child's attention to it. The child may be confused in places that have unfamiliar scents and odors such as in a bakery, in a department store perfume area, and when passing garbage cans on a walk.

Proprioceptive: If two people are available when taking a walk, each person can hold a hand and gently help the child jump over cracks in the sidewalk. At the park, help the child jump from a railroad tie or other very low surface. Once the child's tolerance improves, increase the height of the jump, as the sensory input will be greater.

Tactile: For children who do not like to be confined in a car seat or grocery cart, have a favorite item such as a book, snack, or toy in the seat so that as they are being placed in the seat, they can grab it and focus on something enjoyable. For children who get upset when they feel the wind, prepare them by saying, "Get ready, here comes the wind," and gently blow on their arm to help them understand what is going to happen.

Vestibular: Place the child on a trusted person's lap and introduce very slow and gentle movement. As the child's tolerance increases, gradually decrease the support and increase the excursion of the movement. For very sensitive children, this process may take an extended period of time, although for less sensitive children, the process may occur during one outing.

Visual: Some children react negatively to specific items such as suspended balloons or flags they see in stores. Once items are identified as being a problem for the child, set up similar situations at home where the child is more comfortable. For example, suspend one balloon or flag at home and model a positive affect such as "Wow, how pretty," and if the child is calm, touch the item to cause it to move. If the child shows an interest, allow the child to touch it to make it move.

Diapering and Dressing

It is very difficult to discern whether a child's dislike of diapering and dressing is due to sensory processing factors or whether the child does not want to be disrupted for something that generally is not fun and does not have an immediate payoff. Many children do not mind having a wet or even soiled diaper and do not associate a diaper change with a positive outcome. Giving the child special toys to distract him or her can help make diapering and dressing more tolerable. The items likely will need to be changed frequently, and it is important that they be given to the child before the child begins to fuss and cry so that the fussing and crying are not reinforced. Encourage the child to actively participate in diapering and dressing as much as possible by handing him or her needed items. In addition, encourage the child to assist by physically helping him or her put on and take off clothing, gradually decreasing the assistance. Many children better tolerate the diapering and dressing routine once they understand the purpose, and their participation may help this process.

Tactile and Proprioceptive: Assess to determine if the child better tolerates firm or light touch when cleaning the child during a diaper change. If a specific type of touch is found to be better tolerated, use that type of touch, and once diaper changes improve, gradually vary the pressure to increase the child's acceptance.

Vestibular: Some children do not like to lie down for diapering and dressing. This could be due to vestibular factors, or it could be that the child is in the stage of typical development where this is common. Assessing the child's reaction during dressing and diapering while in a sitting or standing position as opposed to while lying down can help one make this determination.

Grooming and Hygiene

Auditory: Some children dislike haircuts due to the buzzing of clippers and/or the sound of the scissors near their ears. When using clippers, before touching them to the child's hair, turn them on and quickly turn them off several times, keeping them on for longer periods of time. Allow the child to turn them on and off. When using scissors, open and close them repeatedly near the child so he or she can see and hear the scissors. Show the child on a doll or stuffed animal what the scissors will do. Once the child is familiar with them, he or she may better tolerate them near his or her head.

Gustatory and Olfactory: If a child resists toothbrushing, it may be due to the flavor or smell of the toothpaste. Try brushing the child's teeth without toothpaste. Then, over time, if the routine becomes less stressful, put a tiny amount of toothpaste on the brush. Once that amount is tolerated, gradually increase how much toothpaste is on the brush. Try different flavors to perhaps find one the child likes.

Tactile: For children who do not readily tolerate grooming activities such as hair brushing or haircuts, stroke their hair when they are involved in preferred activities such as watching a movie. After they tolerate touch to the hair/head, they may better tolerate haircuts and hair brushing and combing. For toothbrushing, be aware that some teeth may be more sensitive than others and begin with lighter pressure on those teeth until the child is more accepting. Gradually increase the pressure and time spent on those teeth.

Household Activities

Auditory: For a child who finds the sound of the vacuum or hair dryer to be scary or otherwise aversive, give warnings such as verbal and visual cues. These will help the child predict what is going to happen. Allow the child to turn the appliance on and off if there are no safety concerns.

Proprioceptive: Have the child help carry small loads of laundry to and from the washer or dryer, push the vacuum, or carry a watering can to water the plants.

Tactile: Have the child help with laundry, including putting the clothes in and taking the clothes out of the washer and dryer. For children who are able to match, have the child help sort the laundry. When planting seeds or seedlings, have the child dig in the dirt. Wiping up water spills is a good way to encourage children to get their hands wet in a new and purposeful way.

Mealtime/Snack Time

Auditory: If a child dislikes the sound of the mixer, blender, food processor, or microwave timer, give verbal and visual warnings, as discussed earlier in the Household Activities section.

Gustatory and Olfactory: If the child is very sensitive to smells and tends to refuse certain foods after smelling them, expose the child to a variety of smells during other routines. At mealtime, model smelling foods, saying, "Yummy, this smells good," and take a bite, exclaiming how good it tastes.

Tactile and Proprioceptive: Have the child help peel bananas, tear lettuce, shell peas, snap beans, or shake a container to make instant pudding. For children who do not readily touch such items, help the child by providing physical assistance for a very short amount of time, such as peeling the last strand of banana peel or throwing away the peel. As the child gets comfortable, add another small job such as peeling two strands of banana peel or throwing away two food items. If the child does not like to get his or her hands messy, provide forks and spoons and help the child scoop or stab the foods as needed. Always have a napkin, wipe, or cloth nearby so the child can quickly wipe his or her hands.

Visual: Selective eating for children with ASD and related disorders is often related to the appearance of the food. See Chapter 7 for ideas on how to increase acceptance of new foods.

Playtime

Auditory: If a child is fearful or finds toys with sounds to be aversive, playfully activate the toy for a moment and then turn it off or muffle the sound across the room or in another room. As the child becomes accustomed to the sound, play with the toy closer and closer to the child. Be playful by hiding the toy under a blanket and playing Peekaboo with it. Provide opportunities for the child to explore the toy without the sound being activated, and provide opportunities for the child to turn the toy on and off.

Gustatory, Olfactory, and Tactile: Fingerpaint with pudding, ketchup, mustard, whipped topping, and foods the child enjoys. If the child does not want to put his or her hands in the food, place a small amount in a well-sealed plastic bag for the child to manipulate. Once he or she accepts this, place the substance on a cookie sheet and provide a utensil, cotton swab, or unsharpened pencil for the child to use to interact with the substance. Allow the child to play without forcing the child to get his or her hands messy. When the child is having fun, "accidentally" get a tiny amount on the child's hand, say something like "Oops!" and quickly wipe it off. Gradually increase the child's tolerance by "accidentally" putting a little more on the child's hands, taking cues from the child as to readiness for more. Some children need repeated exposures to become comfortable.

Proprioceptive and Vestibular: If two adults are present, swing the child in a sturdy blanket. Take cues from the child as to when to progress from gentle rhythmic motions to irregular motions. If a child does not like to propel ride-on toys, resists being pushed on toys, or resists rocking on a chair or rocking horse, first have the child sit on the item during a preferred activity such as eating a snack, watching a movie, or playing on an electronic tablet. As the child becomes accustomed to the "chair," move it a small amount and gradually increase the amount of movement. For ride-on toys, help the child propel the "bike" forward a foot to obtain a small treat and gradually increase the distance.

Visual: For children who do not like flags, balloons, or other suspended items, playfully toss them to another child or adult away from the child but within sight. Increase the amount of time of the child's exposure and increase the nearness to the child as the child's tolerance increases.

Tips and Hints for Tolerating Sensory Stimuli

It is sometimes difficult to find the fine line between successfully encouraging a child to participate in an activity that he or she finds aversive and forcing a child to do something that will be upsetting. Some children need repeated exposures for very brief amounts of time before they become comfortable.

Make the ending point as predictable as possible. For example, count to 10 very quickly and always stop at 10 so the child knows when the stimulus will be stopped or removed. As the child's tolerance improves, slow the counting.

Ideas for Monitoring Progress: Note new sensory experiences in which the child participates and/or the length of time that the child participates in specific sensory activities.

Shifts Attention

Background Information: Young infants begin to learn the process of taking in information through their senses, focusing on some stimuli while ignoring others, just as older children and adults do throughout their days. During all activities, individuals of all ages must tune out a vast array of sensations in order to participate efficiently. Generally, when sitting and watching television or eating a meal, most people do not typically notice the feeling of their clothing, the sound of the nearby clock ticking, or the aroma of the previous night's dinner, unless those stimuli are particularly aversive or exceptionally pleasurable. Throughout development, exploration leads to the ability to selectively attend to some stimuli while tuning out others. This influences what is perceived, learned, and remembered. What is perceived, learned, and remembered also influences attention in subsequent exploration, making the process dynamic. Selective attention in infants is influenced greatly by aspects of the sensations, including their statistical regularities, intensity, contrast, movement, and redundancy (i.e., information can be gleaned by one sensation though it is perceived by two or more sensations simultaneously). As the infant matures and develops, the child's knowledge, expectations, and goals greatly influence to what stimuli the child attends (Bahrick & Lickliter, 2014). Shifting attention is necessary for learning and participation in nearly all interactions and routines.

Relevance to Children with Autism: The term *sticky fixation* has been used to describe the difficulties young infants have shifting their attention away from visually appealing stimuli (Hood, 1995). Landry and Bryson (2004) related this developmental marker in infants to research findings that showed similar challenges beyond infancy in children with ASD. This term has been expanded, and the term *sticky attention* currently is found in much of the literature regarding ASD and young children. In a review of the literature, Sacrey et al. (2014) found strong evidence that visual disengagement is impaired in ASD and is apparent by 12 months of age. Difficulty shifting attention away from distressing stimuli can affect a young child's emotional and behavioral regulation, and difficulty shifting attention in general can lead to missing a great deal of important social and environmental information. For example, Tamika was so fixated on watching the ceiling fan that she did not hear her mother telling her she would be right back, as she had to run upstairs. A few moments later, Tamika screamed and cried when she noticed her mother was gone. Similarly, when Billy was at his child care center, he spent hours watching the bubbles in the fish tank and missed many opportunities to interact with toys and his peers.

Both Billy and Tamika exhibited difficulties shifting their attention to orient to others. Differences in social orienting are among one of the first symptoms noted in ASD. Very early playful interactions give infants practice in shifting attention, and these interactions are essential to the development of social cognition and the emotional connectedness required for understanding others (Brian, Bryson, & Zwaigenbaum, 2015). Shifting attention is necessary to learn many developmental skills, and the ability to fully participate in routines necessitates the completion of a sequence of actions or behaviors. In order to complete steps, it is necessary to readily shift attention. For example, if a child does not shift attention when playing with a cause-and-effect toy, he or she will not notice the resulting sound or action when pushing the button.

How to Incorporate into Routines: The following are ideas for practicing shifting attention that may fit into a child's routine.

Bath Time

If the child becomes fixated on the running water, position the child so his or her back is to the faucet and create opportunities for interaction such as playfully pouring water from a cup and calling the child's attention by saying "Ready, set, pour" or "Ready, set, go." If the child demonstrates repetitive behaviors in the tub and has difficulty disengaging from an activity, assess the activity to determine the likely sensory stimuli and create a replacement that encourages a shift of attention. For example, if the child is staring at a ceiling fan in the bathroom, blow bubbles or a pinwheel to create a similar visual experience that can be controlled more easily. When washing the child, draw the child's attention to the body part being washed by singing about the body part, patting the body part before washing it, or, if appropriate, kissing or blowing on the body part.

Bedtime

Position the child so he or she can shift attention without being distracted during bedtime interactions such as prayers, songs, kisses, or snuggling. If a fixation or repetitive behavior is calming to the child, it may be appropriate to allow the child to attend to the stimulus to help him or her become drowsy. Conversely, if a sensory stimulus is exciting to the child, modify the environment (e.g., close the bedroom door to dampen sounds in other rooms, turn the fan so it is not blowing directly on the child).

Book Time

Position the child to encourage shifting attention to the reader's face (e.g., the child sits on the sofa and the reader kneels on the floor). Vary the sensory stimuli being targeted, sometimes drawing attention to the pictures and sometimes to the reader's language. Point to the pictures being talked about, tapping them if needed to draw the child's attention. At times, it may be necessary to cover the picture or words momentarily to shift the child's attention to the reader so the child is more likely to attend to the spoken words.

Community Outings

Draw the child's attention to various sensory stimuli such as cars moving, trees swaying in the breeze, cars honking, birds chirping, and the scent of the flowers or freshly cut grass. When at a playground, if the child gets fixated on playing in the tanbark or pulling grass and prefers this type of activity to exploring the playground equipment, try using the preferred sensory stimulus to entice the child to a new activity. For example, if the child is "stuck" playing with the tanbark, roll a handful of tanbark down the slide to help shift the child's attention to the slide. When taking a walk, if the child is hyperfocused on items such as rocks or flowers and wants to gather or throw them, say, "Bye-bye _____; let's go find a _____," thereby saying good-bye to the fixation and redirecting the child to an alternative. If the child is feeling the pine needles in one spot for a prolonged period of time, pick a leaf from a nearby tree and encourage the child to feel it and then direct him or her to the tree from where the leaf was picked.

Diapering and Dressing

Show the child the diaper, the wipes, the ointment, and articles of clothing, naming them. If the child appears to be visually focused on the items but not attending to the names of them, place the item near your mouth to help shift attention to the source of the language. If the child is passive and not assisting with dressing, give cues to help shift the child's attention to the task at hand, ensuring that the child is given enough time to demonstrate the behavior or skill but not so much time that he or she forgets what is expected or gets distracted and moves on. For example, when putting on the child's shoes, if the child does not hold out his or her foot and does not respond to the direction "Give me your foot," tap the child's foot, and if needed, tap the shoe on the floor to make a sound to shift the child's attention to the dressing process so he or she can participate in the first steps toward independence.

Grooming and Hygiene

During hand washing, some children get "stuck" splashing in the water or excessively pumping the soap dispenser and do not shift attention to learn the sequence of the routine. It is helpful to modify the environment or to use prompts and cues to help the child shift attention. For a child who gets stuck playing in the running water, count to five and turn off the water before directing the child to the soap. Over time, the child may independently turn off the water and then reach for the soap or may reach for the soap without turning off the water. If the child tends to pump the soap too many times (i.e., to get proprioceptive, visual, or tactile feedback), move the soap dispenser out of his or her reach and, if needed, give verbal or visual cues to help shift the child's attention to the next step of the process.

Household Activities

Allow and help the child to participate in activities such as doing laundry, rinsing unbreak-able dishes, pushing a vacuum, and watering plants to provide numerous opportunities for shifting attention.

Mealtime/Snack Time

Self-feeding involves many episodes of shifting attention. A child must shift attention to his or her food, utensil, and cup in order to perform the needed motor sequence. Meal-time offers many opportunities for social interaction, and to participate, a child must shift attention to others. Many families get into the habit of using television, movies, or apps to get through mealtime, using the electronics to establish regulation. Over time, however, this becomes a habit that can interfere not only with the development of independence, but also with mealtime interactions. When the family is ready, a plan that is sensitive to the whole family's needs and style can be developed to wean the child from electronic distractions.

Playtime

Playtime is laden with opportunities to shift attention and encourage engagement. Play sensory-social games and pause to facilitate shifting of attention and a glance to your eyes (see Chapter 8). Position yourself so the child can easily shift from what he or she is doing to look at what you are doing. If the child is demonstrating play that is repetitive, use the child's sensory and activity preferences to shift attention. Model actions and sounds that will capture the child's attention and motivation and that are related to the play. For example, if the child is crawling, bark like a dog or meow like a cat, or if the child is opening and closing the door on a toy, knock on the door and say "Knock, knock."

Tips and Hints for Shifting Attention

Be aware of the position of the child and the stimulus that the child needs to shift toward. Begin by making it as easy as possible for the child to shift attention and then gradually increase the challenge. For example, when the goal is for a child to look at an item presented during a routine, at first bring an item the child likes into his or her visual field and excitedly say "Look!" Over time, informally, but systematically, decrease the intensity of the affect of the word *look* and use less preferred items to help the child learn to look toward items shown.

If a child is having difficulty shifting attention in order to participate in an activity, discern what sensory system is being stimulated and for what purpose. If the child is throwing objects, determine whether the child appears to be seeking visual input, auditory input, or both by looking at the child's preferences for objects thrown, whether the child is intently watching the objects, and/or whether the child appears to be more focused on the sound. To help shift the child's attention to facilitate engagement, join the child by imitating him or her and then modify the activity to be more purposeful by throwing objects that will have the desired sensory feedback into a box or laundry basket. If the child mouths toys instead of putting them in the container, try a sensory substitute such as allowing the child to have a teething toy when working on container play. If the child is not interested in the sensory substitute, the substitute may not be similar enough to what the child is seeking or the child may be avoiding the task and using the sensory seeking behavior because it is more enjoyable. In situations where it is difficult to motivate the child, it is often helpful to use sensory seeking behaviors as a reward for less motivating activities (e.g., help the child put the object into the container and then allow the child to put the toy in his or her mouth for the count of 10; counting helps the child anticipate when the opportunity to mouth the toy will be over).

Use cues that are helpful for the individual child's sensory system and developmental level to shift attention. For example, some children respond well to a tap on the arm along with a verbal direction to "Look at the _____," whereas those who are hypersensitive to touch or who do not understand the intent of the touch may go into a flight-or-fight response. For children who respond negatively to touch, an auditory cue such as a high affect exclamation and placement of the item within the child's visual field is likely to better shift the child's attention (e.g., "Wow! Look at this _____.").

Pace the flow to the child's needs and avoid bombarding the child with demands of frequent attention shifting.

In some situations, such as when a child is not regulated or is likely to become upset, it may not be appropriate to address shifting attention. For example, in a restaurant, if the goal is for the family to successfully eat a meal with the child remaining seated at the table without screaming, initially it may be appropriate for the child to play with his or her tablet or an app on the parent's phone. Once the child is able to sit calmly, which might be during the first trip to the restaurant or perhaps during the third or fourth, the next goal can be for the child to participate in new ways that entail shifting attention and becoming more aware of the environment.

Difficulty shifting attention is often due to competing reinforcers. In other words, what the child is supposed to shift to is not as pleasurable as what he or she is doing. It is therefore necessary to entice the child to shift attention to the important stimuli by making the target as rewarding and motivating as possible.

Many children with ASD have difficulty initiating in a variety of situations, including in communication and in play. This may be related to shifting attention and motor planning. To help children initiate, it is beneficial for the child to have access to choices. For example, provide options of snacks from which the child can choose. At first, have each snack item in a clear container so the child can see the options. Later, progress to leaving the snacks in their package to help the child move toward more abstract thinking. Some children do not readily initiate getting toys or books from where they are kept yet will choose one when several are placed in a novel spot where they are easily seen. When children have easy access to toys, books, or household objects such as spoons and bowls, they often will use them rather than engaging in self-stimulatory behaviors. Show the child a variety of ways to play with them to give the child ideas that will lead to initiation and playing independently. Rotate which toys and objects are available to help prevent satiation and boredom.

Ideas for Monitoring Progress: Note the number of times in a number of opportunities the child turns to a visual or auditory presentation within a given routine, such as the number of times Kevin looked when five peers said "hi" to him or the number of times Suzy looked at the 10 different pictures her mother pointed to during book time.

Imitates Actions

Background Information: Young et al. (2011) described imitation as "a critical component of the profound social and intellectual development" that occurs in infancy and toddlerhood when a child learns to imitate actions, sounds, and words and as part of the "continuous process of learning about the world and negotiating complex social relationships" (p. 1565). For many years, research has focused on imitation in infants as both a precursor to and a product of increased sociocognitive competence (Dunphy-Lelii, LaBounty, Lane, & Wellman, 2014).

Relevance to Children with Autism: Infants and toddlers with autism demonstrate less imitative behavior than do typically developing children, and although these abilities improve over time, imitation difficulties persist in many individuals (Vivanti & Hamilton, 2014). In their review of the literature, Vivanti and Hamilton found that individuals with autism more easily imitate actions with objects than actions without objects, when they are familiar with the materials, when they understand the goals of the person modeling the task, and when the outcome of the task is of interest. In a study comparing preschoolers with autism, preschoolers with global developmental delays, and preschoolers who were developing typically, Vivanti, Trembath, and Dissanayake (2014) found that those with autism imitated less frequently than children in the other two groups, and when they imitated, their movements were less accurate than those of typically developing children.

How to Incorporate into Routines: The following are ideas for practicing imitation skills that may fit into a child's routine.

Bath Time

Model gentle splashing actions with bath toys such as having the duck, fish, or superhero swim through the water, blowing suds off a surface, or washing easily reached body parts. Once the child can imitate many actions, progress to modeling actions that require more visual attention (e.g., washing the wrist or a specific finger) and actions that require motor sequencing and two steps (e.g., making the rubber duck swim and then fly).

Bedtime

Bedtime opportunities for imitation include giving goodnight kisses and hugs to family members and stuffed animals and folding hands for bedtime prayers.

Book Time

When looking at or reading books, model actions that are relevant to the pictures (e.g., smelling flowers, eating food, hopping like a rabbit). If the child does not imitate, help him or her to do so. High-affect exclamations may also elicit verbalizations. (See Chapter 8.)

Community Outings

When taking walks, blow dandelions, jump over sidewalk cracks, walk on railroad ties, smell flowers, or fly like a bird and tell the child "You do" or "Your turn." At the grocery store, put several apples in the bag, hand the child an apple, and have the bag ready to catch the apple as the child places it in or tries unsuccessfully to toss it. At the park, roll a ball up or down the slide for the child to imitate. At the pond, throwing food to the fish or to the ducks can be a fun way to elicit imitation, as the wildlife's response may be very motivating.

Diapering and Dressing

Play Peekaboo when taking off the child's shirt, repeating the action and language several times. Place the shirt on top of the child's head, partially covering the eyes to try to elicit an imitation of the game. Some children love when parents or other caregivers smell their feet, playfully make a face, pretend the feet smell terrible, and exclaim, "Phew, stinky feet," and will imitate smelling their feet, making the face, and/or exclaiming "Phew" when the feet are placed near the child's nose.

Grooming and Hygiene

When helping the child with washing and drying his or her hands and face, as well as when helping to brush teeth or comb hair, perform the needed actions a few times, pause, and wait to see if the child imitates the actions. Use verbal cues and physical prompts and fade them once the child begins to imitate.

Household Activities

Involve the child in activities such as watering plants, sweeping the floor, mopping the floor, rinsing the dishes, putting napkins on the table, wiping the table, and putting laundry in the dryer, as there are numerous opportunities to facilitate imitation by pausing after a few repetitions.

Mealtime/Snack Time

During mealtime or snack time preparation, the child can imitate shaking plastic bottles of salad dressing, stirring cold sauces, pouring into a bowl, spreading jam with a butter knife, or serving food onto a plate.

Playtime

Imitation can be integrated into any play activity such as banging, shaking, dumping, throwing, kicking, filling, pushing buttons, building, and pretending. Put a toy on your head, pretend to sneeze, and tip your head forward so the toy falls to the floor. Repeat this several times and then put the toy on the child's head, as this often results in the child performing the action for the effect of the drop as well as a sharing of affect. If the child repeats the action after you put the toy on his or her head, try handing the child the toy to see if he puts it on his or her own head or yours.

Tips and Hints for Imitating Actions

Some children spontaneously perform an action and/or follow a direction to perform the action but do not imitate the action. For example, Lila clapped her hands when excited and when her mother told her to do so, but she did not clap when others clapped and was unable to clap when her mother clapped and told her "You do." For children who do not readily imitate, begin with simple actions in their motor repertoire (e.g., clapping, blowing a kiss) as well as actions with objects (e.g., building with blocks, putting objects in a container) so they can be physically assisted if necessary. Some children need specific intervention to help them understand the expectation of imitation. Lila's mother taught Lila to clap using the phrase "You do." Initially Lila thought "You do" was synonymous with the direction "Clap your hands." Her mother discovered this when she modeled blowing a kiss and told Lila "You do" and then Lila clapped her hands. When such a misunderstanding occurs, it is helpful to teach the child to imitate several different actions so he or she learns "You do" means imitate.

Assess if the child more readily imitates peers or adults and initially try to provide models that are more likely to facilitate imitation.

As with other skills, begin where the child is most successful and work toward generalization and expansion of the frequency of imitation, the variety of imitation, and the complexity of imitation.

Be sure the action modeled fits into the family or child care setting. For example, imitating drumming with spoons on pots and pans might not be an activity a family wants to encourage. Similarly, kicking cardboard blocks may not be acceptable in a child care setting.

Ideas for Monitoring Progress: Note the items imitated during specific routines, number of items the child imitated during specific routines, number of times the child imitated in a given time period, and/or number of times the child imitated peers in a given time period or routine.

Follows Directions

Background Information: In order to follow directions, one must attend to the direction, comprehend the message, and be able and willing to complete the necessary action or actions. Following directions enables participation in activities that facilitate learning about the physical and social world.

Relevance to Children with Autism: Children with ASD may not follow directions due to a lack of attention, comprehension, and/or motivation. Difficulty following directions affects participation in family routines and limits learning opportunities. It is necessary for EI providers to help families and other caregivers determine which factors are interfering with the ability to follow directions in order to target them appropriately so the child is successful in a variety of settings and situations.

How to Incorporate into Routines: The following are ideas for practicing following directions that may fit into a child's routine.

Bath Time

Tell the child to get a towel, put clothes in the hamper, sit down, stand up, clean up the bath toys, and give you a body part such as his or her hand or foot.

Bedtime

Tell the child to climb in bed, give you a kiss, get a book, put the book away, turn on the light, and say "night-night."

Book Time

Tell the child to go get a book (any book) or to go get the _____ book (specific book), put it away, give it to you, turn the page, and touch the picture of the _____.

Community Outings

When leaving the house: Tell the child to get your shoes/jacket, turn off the light, open the door, and close the door.

At the grocery store: Tell the child to put it in, hold the cart, give to you, and give you the _____.

At the park: Tell the child to run, jump, kick, throw, come to you, and go down the slide.

On a walk: Tell the child to hold your hand, jump, find a leaf, wave hi to the truck, and point to the stop sign.

Outings in the car: Tell the child to climb in, climb out, put an arm through (the car seat harness), and wave hi or bye.

Dressing and Diapering

Tell the child to lie down, hold the wipe, give you the diaper, put it in the trash, stand up, take off socks, give you a foot, give you the shirt, and sit down.

Grooming and Hygiene

Tell the child to step up on the stool, get some soap, turn on/off the water, rub hands, dry hands, wash face, get the toothbrush, and brush hair.

Household Activities

Tell the child to turn off the vacuum, get the broom, throw it away, and give you the remote.

Mealtime/Snack Time

Tell the child to take a bite, get the _____ (from the plate or cupboard), use the fork, and scoop with the spoon.

Playtime

Tell the child to put in, put on, make it go, get the _____, feed the bear, make bear go night-night, make the car go, roll the ball, throw it in, make the airplane fly, put the man in the truck, roll the dough, and go dot-dot-dot (with a crayon or marker).

Tips and Hints for Following Directions

When targeting direction following, consider comprehension, willingness or compliance, and motor sequencing abilities. For children who struggle with receptive language, use few words and provide meaningful visual cues such as gestures or pictures. Use decreasing prompts (see Chapter 3) and fade them so the child becomes independent. For example, at snack time on his first day in his new child care setting, Julio's EI provider showed his teacher how to take the cereal bar to where Julio was playing, show it to him, and then head toward the table, telling him "Come eat." As Julio approached the table, his EI provider patted his chair and said, "Sit down." After several days, Julio did not need the prompts of being shown the food or patting the chair, as he followed the directions "Come eat" and "Sit down" independently. To build success as quickly as possible and to avoid unnecessary frustration, one must use the hierarchy of skills that is followed by children who are developing typically. For example, in typical development, children follow two-step related directions before two-step unrelated ones, and understanding of possessives, pronouns, and number concepts develops in the later months of toddlerhood. In addition, a child who does not yet demonstrate understanding of each component skill would not be able to "Get two of sister's green socks from the laundry basket in Mommy's room." Following multistep directions involves not only comprehension of each step but also memory and the ability to filter distractions.

Avoid language that gives a choice such as "Can you?" "Will you?" or "Do you want to?" when the child does not have a choice. Instead, simply state the direction so that the child learns that there is an expectation.

Tell the child what to do rather than what not to do in order to help teach a replacement behavior as well as to make the language as simple as possible. Many toddlers, including those without language processing problems, do not understand negatives, so when they hear "Don't climb on the table," they often climb on the table.

To help a child comprehend the language involved in a direction, give the direction just as he or she is about to perform the action. For example, as the child pushes the door closed, say "Shut the door," or as the child brings a sandwich to his or her mouth, say "Take a bite."

For a child who is very self-directed and/or who becomes dysregulated when demands are placed upon him or her, begin with a direction that is quick, is easy, and can be physically prompted (e.g., "Give me five."). Take advantage of the child's motivation when he or she is very clear about what he or she wants. For example, if the child communicates verbally or nonverbally that he or she wants to get down from the highchair after eating, tell the child "First give me a high-five and then you may get down." If the child does not give a high-five, help him or her do so and then quickly take the child out of the highchair. Once a child learns a direction in a given routine, generalize the skill to other routines and also begin new directions in the initial routine. This helps to prevent the direction from becoming a rote response that does not require listening skills.

At first, target following directions when the child is happy and calm and with materials that foster regulation. For example, if a child likes bubbles and calmly watches as others blow them, catching one on the wand and telling him or her to pop it might work well, as there are opportunities for fun practice. Conversely, if the child runs wildly through the house or cries whenever he or she sees bubbles, it is wise to choose a different activity in which to embed a new direction.

Find opportunities to use "first–then" language to build compliance, emphasizing the preferred opportunity in hopes of avoiding a battle of wills. For example, if a child is told to clean up and then he can watch a movie, instead of using a demanding, dictatorial tone of voice emphasizing the direction "*First clean up,* then movie," say "*Sure, you may have movie.* First clean up, then movie." Similarly, if the child wants to play on a tablet, say, "First sit down, then *tablet,*" emphasizing the word "tablet."

When introducing new directions, arrange the environment to reduce distractions and embed opportunities for repetition and success. For example, when first teaching a child to clean up blocks, hand the child one block at a time and say "Clean up," placing the bin beneath his or her hand to make it as easy as possible. Over time, decrease prompts by using visual cues such as pointing to the block and/or the bin rather than handing the child the block and then fade the assistance until the child is independent.

Identify directions that will be functional and allow multiple opportunities in a week for practice, such as "Get your shoes" before going outside, "Sit down" before eating, "Wave bye-bye" when a parent leaves for work, "Put your cup on the table" when the child is finished drinking, and "Turn off the water" when washing hands before eating.

Give a direction twice, and if the child does not do it, help him or her. A child who understands the direction and chooses not to do it will often comply when told "Do it or I will help you."

If it is very likely that the child will not follow a direction and it is impossible to help the child to do so, avoid giving the direction so that noncompliance is not reinforced.

Choose directions and the timing of directions with care. Consider whether the direction is important, the likelihood that it will be followed, and whether it is worth helping the child follow through at that time. If targeting compliance, use directions that the child comprehends. If targeting understanding of language, the child must be compliant. If the child is very tired, very hungry, or otherwise dysregulated, avoid giving directions that are challenging. (See Chapter 5.)

If considering using a sequence of pictures to help a child follow directions, such as steps to hand washing posted near the bathroom sink, one must assess whether the child understands what each picture represents. If a child does not associate the pictures with the actions he or she must perform, the pictures will not be useful. This is true for all representations, whether they are words, gestures, or pictures. The child must make an association before the word, gesture, or picture will be meaningful. In some instances, visual supports can be very helpful, but they may need to be taught.

Ideas for Monitoring Progress: Note new directions the child follows, the number of directions the child follows within specific routines, the types of prompts the child needs to follow directions, the type of direction the child follows (i.e., one-step familiar, one-step novel, two-step related, two-step unrelated), and/or new vocabulary and new concepts demonstrated in directions.

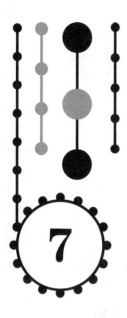

Building Skills to Support Flexibility

7

The ability to adapt to changes and to accommodate and assimilate across people, experiences, and routines supports regulated responses to typical changes that occur on a daily basis. Infants and toddlers must adapt to changes as they interact with multiple caregivers, as they participate in routines, and as their bodies change and skills develop. In addition, cognitive flexibility develops, which requires shifting attention, responding, holding information in the mind, and inhibiting other distractions and other responses in order to attain a goal. These processes make it possible for children to make predictions and act upon their world (Forssman, 2012).

It is well documented that individuals with ASD have trouble adapting to demands of the environment, show rigid behavior, hold on to previous behavior patterns, have restricted and repetitive behaviors, have a strong preference for consistency, and show difficulty in adapting to changing plans or alterations of their routine in daily life (D'Cruz et al., 2013; Kanner, 1943). Criteria listed in the *DSM-5* include "restricted and repetitive patterns of behavior," and examples cited include items related to Flexibility, including "insistence on sameness," "inflexible adherence to routines," "ritualized patterns of verbal or nonverbal behavior," and "highly restricted, fixated interests that are abnormal in intensity or focus" (APA, 2013, p. 50).

Theories regarding the causes of inflexibility in ASD are varied and include challenges with sensory processing as well as difficulties understanding others' intents. The latter has been associated with anxiety in individuals with ASD and termed *intolerance of uncertainty*. Some believe restricted and repetitive behaviors are strategies used to make life predictable (Boulter, Freeston, South, & Rodgers, 2014). Cognitive flexibility, the ability to shift actions and thoughts to meet the demands of situations, has been noted to be impaired in most individuals with ASD. Though not considered to be a core deficit, cognitive inflexibility explains difficulties with transitions and changes in routines (Leung & Zakzanis, 2014).

EI providers are frequently asked to help parents and other caregivers with a child's behavioral challenges regarding a lack of Flexibility. A lack of Flexibility can affect any or all daily routines, including a child's insistence on the same clothing, foods, schedule, route to the park, television shows, or others' responses in specific situations. A mother who has multiple children with autism was asked to reflect back on what she wished she had learned when her children were in EI, and she responded,

> Flexibility is the key. I think they need to try to combat the flexibility early. I know parents of children in kindergarten who STILL take their kids to Taco Bell each afternoon

before dropping them off or else the child melts down. I mean these routines RULE the family, RULE the household. If you know the child likes something like going the "long" way in the neighborhood, you need to work on going the short way. I think if we let the children become too embedded in routines and inflexibility it carries on forever and leads to meltdowns, behaviors, parents walking on eggshells, etc. Flexibility should be a goal, like if the child only plays with red Legos make them play with blue during your session. Teach parents how to deal with the inflexible child and help to change it. I think rigidity of thought plays so much into things. I mean look they become rigid on being first and winning as well. (Personal communication, June 17, 2014)

Temple Grandin, a well-known author and college professor who is on the autism spectrum, agrees:

> How can common sense be taught? I think it starts with teaching flexibility at a young age. Structure is good for children with autism, but sometimes plans can, and need to be, changed. When I was little, my nanny made my sister and me do a variety of activities. This variety prevented rigid behavior patterns from forming. I became more accustomed to changes in our daily or weekly routines and learned that I could still manage when change occurred. (Grandin, 2002)

How to Incorporate into Routines: Some children with ASD are quite flexible, whereas others are not. In addition, some children are quite adaptable in some situations but inflexible in others. The following strategies are ideas for incorporating changes into routines that can be implemented gradually and playfully to aid in promoting Flexibility for children who tend to be rigid. Implementing too many changes at once would likely overwhelm both the child and the caregiver. These suggestions are ideas to introduce at a pace that is comfortable for the child and the family. If challenging behaviors occur when implementing these strategies, a careful analysis is needed to determine the causes and solutions.

Bath Time

When convenient and practical, have bath time at a different time of day or in a different bathroom. Vary the order in which the child is washed. Give the child a choice whereby both choices are different from the usual routine. For example, if the child's face is usually washed first, ask him or her, "Do you want to wash your hands or your ears first?" Use a variety of colors of towels and washcloths. Use a variety of language, not only to increase Flexibility, but also to build vocabulary. For example, use the verbs *wash* and *clean* interchangeably.

Bedtime

Give the child a choice of two books to read, two songs to sing, or two prayers to say that are both a change from the routine. Vary the closure when leaving the room (e.g., "Night-night," "Sleep tight," "See you in the morning").

Book Time

When looking at books, sometimes talk about the pictures and sometimes read the text. Vary the questions asked about the pictures or the story. Because many children with autism have difficulty responding to language presented in novel ways due to challenges related to how they process language, vary how questions are asked. For example, for children who know animals and animal sounds, ask "What does the cow say?" as well as "Which one says 'moo'?"

Community Outings

Vary the route when going for walks. Sometimes take a stroller or wagon and sometimes have the child walk. Distract the child—before he or she has time to resist—by looking for flowers, numbers on the mailbox, or other items of interest to the child. When driving to familiar places, vary the route. If safe and practical, sometimes change the location of the child's safety seat in the car. For example, on occasion, he or she can sit next to a different sibling or on the opposite side of the car. If the child watches movies while riding in the car, vary the selection and at times have movie-free excursions. Similarly, vary songs sung and types of music played. If multiple adults or older children go to the grocery store, it is important that the same person is not always the one pushing the cart. For stores that have multiple types of carts (e.g., those that resemble cars as well as typical grocery carts), vary the type of cart in which the child rides.

Diapering and Dressing

Vary where the child's diaper is changed and where the child is dressed. Vary the order in which clothes are put on and taken off.

Grooming and Hygiene

When it is time to replace items such as toothbrushes, toothpaste, and soap, choose different flavors, scents, colors, and other relevant attributes. On occasion, change the timing of the routine or the setting of the routine.

Household Activities

Modeling Flexibility during household chores can help demonstrate that changes in routines are acceptable.

Mealtime/Snack Time

Because difficulties with eating are common in children with autism and because these challenges create a great deal of stress for families, this topic is presented in detail later in this chapter.

Playtime

Encourage using toys in new ways. If the child always builds a block tower, make a train of blocks. If the child feeds a stuffed bear with a spoon, model feeding the bear with a fork. Play with balls by rolling, kicking, throwing to a person, and knocking over water bottles. When singing songs that have multiple verses, such as "The Wheels on the Bus," vary the order in which the verses are sung.

Tips and Hints to Support Flexibility in Routines

If a child exhibits a lack of Flexibility in object use, expand the child's repertoire by finding a more acceptable substitute. For example, if the child spins, play Ring Around the Rosy or provide a toy such as a Sit 'n Spin. If the child drops items to watch them fall, provide toys and activities that have a strong visual component, such as one in which a ball or figure rolls down a ramp.

To help children make transitions, use preferred items to help them want to move to another activity. For example, to help a child get out of the bathtub, hold a favorite toy just outside the tub so that he or she will be more likely to want to get out. Similarly, leave a favorite toy in the car to help a child leave the playground. Focus on what the child will do next rather than on what the child is leaving. For example, say "Let's go get your bunny—he's waiting for you in the car" rather than "It is time to go home."

Saying good-bye often helps children make a transition. For example, when a child does not want to leave the toy area in the store, say "Bye toys—see you next time." Many children learn this strategy and spontaneously and calmly say good-bye to objects and situations.

Give a warning a short time before the transition occurs. The warning should be as concrete as possible, such as "One more time down the slide, then we'll go get your cup," as opposed to an abstract warning that contains a time concept the child does not understand, such as "We are leaving in 3 minutes." It is important that the warning be adhered to even if the child is having a tantrum so the tantrum does not lead to good things happening, which will likely increase tantrum behavior.

When moving from one activity to another, distract the child by making the transition fun, such as by counting steps, saying the alphabet, singing a song, or jumping the child from one place to the next.

If a child perseverates on numbers and letters or has other fixations that interfere with inter-action or participation in routines, it is often helpful to begin using the child's interest as a starting point and then expand slowly. For example, Bella did not use any words but began to name letters while watching her alphabet video. Her parents noticed she could name let-ters in books and on her blocks, though they had not taught her to do so. She did not name pictures or point to named pictures. Her EI provider began by using Bella's interest in letters to teach her to point to named pictures. During sessions, Bella's mother would tell Bella to touch a letter and then would take her finger to help Bella point. After a few sessions, Bella could point to named letters without prompts. The next step was to use pictures from the video to teach Bella to point to pictures. The provider found pictures similar to those presented with each letter in the video, and she showed Bella's mother how to gradually introduce pointing to pictures during their routine of pointing to letters. After several weeks, Bella was able to point to the named pictures from her video. Her mother then began to introduce pointing to named pictures in Bella's books.

As discussed in Chapter 3, teaching for generalization is necessary for functional skill devel-opment and because children with autism often focus on irrelevant stimuli, which can result not only in a lack of generalization but also in impaired learning. Often children with autism appear quite rigid, wanting to do something the way they did it the first and subsequent times. Embedding variety into daily routines can be helpful in fostering Flexibility. Con-versely, however, there are times when Flexibility is not the priority in a specific routine, such as when introducing a new skill when inconsistencies would be confusing.

Some children are rigid about others' roles. For example, Alexa had a tantrum if her father came in her room in the morning to get her out of her crib and if he pushed the grocery cart, though she was calm when her mother performed these routines. Her parents com-pared notes and could not determine any discernible differences in their techniques that would lead them to believe the issues were sensory related. Some parents are comfortable with the method of ignoring the tantrums; others prefer an approach they think is less stressful that involves gradually getting the child accustomed to changes. Alexa's parents preferred the more gentle approach and decided that her father would get her out of the crib and hand her to her mother. Over time, Alexa's mother moved farther and farther from the crib until she was no longer in the room. Similarly, in the grocery store, her father pushed Alexa in the cart while counting to 10 very quickly and then her mother took over. Gradually, her father counted more slowly, and Alexa became accustomed to him pushing the cart.

Inflexibility Related to Eating

Inflexibility at mealtime is a particularly challenging routine that necessitates a more in-depth discussion and more explicit strategies. The following vignettes illustrate commonly observed scenarios.

Jessica ate pureed fruits from pouches but refused to eat when her mother poured the food from the pouch into the bowl. Her mother knew she liked the food, so she touched the food to her daughter's lips. Jessica screamed, spit it out, screamed "Yuck," and fussed for 5 minutes despite her routine of eating the same food from the pouch several times a week without any aversive reactions. Mohammed ate his cereal from a green bowl every day. One day his mother did not get a chance to wash it, so she put the cereal in a blue bowl that was identical in size and material, and Mohammed threw it across the room. Eliza ate French fries from a particular fast-food restaurant but not the ones her mother cooked at home. When her mother put the homemade ones in the restaurant package, Eliza picked up a fry, turned it to examine each of its sides, smelled it, and left the table. Dominica was playing with her favorite doll. Her teacher told the class that it was time for snack. Dominica looked to see what food was being placed on the table and continued to play with her doll even after her teacher called her three times.

It is well documented in the literature that food selectivity is commonly found in young children, and children with autism often have more pronounced selectivity (Kerwin, Eicher, & Gelsinger, 2005; Schmitt, Heiss, & Campbell, 2008; Schreck, Williams, & Smith, 2004; Williams, Hendy, & Knecht, 2008). Ahearn, Castine, Nault, and Green (2001) theorized that selective eating may be a "manifestation of the restricted interests and activities" seen in autism (p. 510). Food selectivity can be related to taste, texture, or smell, but in the authors' experience, food selectivity in toddlers and preschoolers is often related to the children's preference for visual sameness. Once rigid behaviors occur, it is often challenging to change routines. Resistance to making a transition to the table may be another challenge related to mealtime. For some children, transitions are difficult because they do not know what is coming next, often due to language comprehension challenges. Other children, like Dominica, resist changing from a preferred activity to a less preferred activity, referred to by some as an issue of competing reinforcers.

Tips and Hints for Inflexibility Related to Eating

If a child has significant feeding challenges and the child's health and nutrition are affected, it is important that medical issues be ruled out before these strategies are implemented. In addition, if an EI provider finds that these strategies are ineffective, he or she may want to further evaluate to ensure that the function (or functions) of the behavior has been determined. Children who have significant eating issues often need help from professionals (e.g., behavior analysts, occupational therapists, speech-language pathologists) who have expertise in feeding disorders.

On occasion, change the location of the child's highchair, booster seat, or chair. Playfully give the child a choice of two new options, for example "Let's be silly today. You can move your chair next to Mommy or next to your brother!"

Playtime can be used to expose picky eaters to new foods in a setting that is often less stressful than mealtime or snack time. Instead of finger painting with paints, use ketchup, mustard, pudding, or other foods the child may like. For children who do not like to touch sticky substances, provide a cotton swab, a coffee stirrer, a craft stick, or other safe item to serve as a "paintbrush." Playfully model making dots and circles and then lick your finger or the paintbrush without telling the child to do so. If other children who follow directions well are part of the activity, have them lick their fingers or paintbrushes and praise them. For another activity, provide dry cereal for sensory play involving scooping, filling, and dumping, and add an appropriate new food type such as a new type of dry cereal the child does not yet eat, or blueberries, or perhaps cooked peas. At first, have the goal that the child will touch the new food. Model scooping, pouring, and picking up the new food and placing it into a cup or bowl. Later, enthusiastically taste the new food without telling the child to do so, and encourage any peers or siblings who are participating to taste the new food, enthusiastically praising them when they take a taste. Similarly, provide new food to make shapes, figures, numbers, or letters that the child enjoys. For example, use dry cereal to make a face and then playfully eat the nose, then an eye. Ask the child if he or she wants to eat a nose. If the child does so, move to a different type of preferred food and repeat the activity. When this is successful, try the activity with a new food.

During mealtime and snack time, change the presentation of foods that are in the child's repertoire. For example, if the child eats sandwiches, cut them in various shapes and sizes. Vary the color and size of the plates and bowls. Change one property at a time to move to new foods. For example, if the child eats only pink yogurt from the container, present the same yogurt in a different container or a different yogurt in the pink yogurt's container. Once the new presentation is well accepted, move to another small change, such as a different brand's pink yogurt in an accepted dish and then later in a novel dish. If the child eats fish-shaped crackers, present different flavors of them. Slightly vary the temperatures of food and drinks. If the milk is typically warmed for 30 seconds, warm for 28 seconds one time and for 31 seconds the next time.

Involve the child in cooking and meal preparation by having him or her tear lettuce, stir cold foods, pour, and participate in similar safe activities. Playfully taste the foods and express delight without telling the child to taste the food. If the child tastes the food, praise him or her. Often when a child is allowed to experiment on his or her own at times other than mealtime, he or she will be more likely to taste a food. When the child is seated at the table or in his or her booster seat, perhaps while the meal is being prepared, present some food items to put in and out of containers or sort. Having a few pieces of a preferred food and a few pieces of a new food that differ only slightly from the preferred food in terms of color, texture, or shape may encourage the child to taste a new food. Providing play opportunities such as these when the child is hungry can be beneficial.

Use successive approximations and shaping to help move the child from accepting a new food on his or her plate or tray to eating the new food. For children who follow directions well, first present one or two small pieces of the new food on the child's plate or tray. If the child becomes upset, allow him or her to hand the food back to you or put it in a bowl. This is an important step for children who are resistant to touching a new food item. Provide several opportunities to do this until the child readily touches the food. Once the child accepts touching the food, work on having him or her accept the food on the plate or highchair tray. Tell the child, "I'll count to 10, and then you can put it in the bowl (or give it to me)." At first, count quickly, and after several opportunities to practice, count more slowly to increase the time of acceptance. After several mealtimes with the new food presented without difficulty, use the Premack (1959) principle of "First _____, then _____," where "first" can refer to kissing the food and "then" can refer to a special treat or the child's opportunity to leave the table to play. Many children will not pick up the food to kiss it, so it will likely be necessary for the parent or provider to touch the child's lips very quickly, make a kissing sound, and reward with the treat or allow the child to leave the table. If a small treat is used (e.g., a chocolate chip, a piece of cookie), multiple opportunities likely will be available during that meal. Often a child resists the first several times and then eagerly allows the item to touch his or her lips to get the treat or leave the table to play. After several meals using this strategy, change the requirement to licking the new food. Because one cannot easily help the child lick the food, the reward cannot be the opportunity to leave the table to play because if the child refuses, the adult is in the very undesirable position of strengthening the child's refusal behaviors. Therefore, at this stage in the process, a treat, whether it be food or a special activity, must be the reward. After several successful meals, the requirement can be changed to "Take a tiny bite," whereby, again, a treat of a food or opportunity must be used rather than the opportunity to leave the table. If the child refuses either at the licking stage or the taking a bite stage, he or she does not get the reward. It is important that the provider or parent not cajole the child into licking or taking a bite, as often this results in the child getting a lot of attention for refusing. Conversely, however, it is very important that the provider or caregiver enthusiastically praise the desired behaviors of touching the food, kissing the food, licking the food, and especially taking bites. On occasion, some children figure out that they can put the food in their mouths, get the treat, and then spit out the food. To alleviate this, for the first several bites, reward the child when he or she puts the food in his or her mouth, but then quickly change the requirement to swallowing the food.

For children who do not follow directions well, the introduction of new foods can be accomplished successfully by using positive reinforcement. It is important to first identify several strong reinforcers (see Chapter 3). Give the child a taste of a preferred food and, as soon as the child takes a bite, reinforce the child's acceptance of the food with a preferred item or activity (e.g., bubbles, a straw to place in an empty water bottle, a phrase from a favorite song, an enthusiastic high-five). Present a tiny bite of the new food. Reinforce the child's acceptance of the new food with the preferred item or activity if the bite is taken. Present three bites of the preferred food and reinforce each bite eaten. Again present a tiny bite of the new or nonpreferred food. Reinforce the behavior of taking a bite if the child does so. If successful, increase the size of the nonpreferred food and alternate bites of preferred and nonpreferred. Over time, continue to increase the size of the new food until it is a typically sized bite for the child and increase the number of presentations at a given meal or snack time. Gradually fade the reinforcer by increasing the number of bites before the reinforcer is given. This technique often works best at snack time because it is quite intensive and can disrupt a family mealtime.

Ideas for Monitoring Progress: Make a list of ways the child adapted to variations in specific routines and/or the number of changes the child adapted to in specific routines.

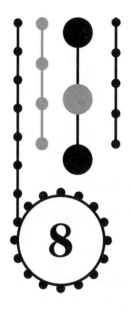

Building Skills to Support Social Communication

8

Social Communication is the ability to use "language in interpersonally appropriate ways to influence people and interpret events" (Olswang, Coggins, & Timler, 2001, p. 51). Although definitions of Social Communication may differ, there is agreement in the literature that Social Communication involves the integration of several components: social interaction, language processing, pragmatics, and social cognition (Adams, 2005).

Social interaction involves reciprocity, or turn-taking, and incorporates joint and shared attention across different people, places, routines, and activities. Joint attention, as discussed in Chapter 4, is composed of RJA (responding to joint attention) and IJA (initiating joint attention). RJA refers to following the direction of a gaze or gesture of others in order to attend to and share a point of reference, and IJA refers to the use of gestures and eye contact to call attention to oneself, objects, actions, or events (Mundy & Jarrold, 2010). According to Mundy and Newell (2007), joint attention is "an expression of the exquisitely honed human capacity to coordinate attention with a social partner, which is fundamental to our aptitude for learning, language, and sophisticated social competencies throughout life" (p. 269).

Language processing involves the comprehension and production of language and may involve speech, gestures, and/or augmentative communication to convey messages and the understanding of both verbal and nonverbal language. Another component of Social Communication, pragmatic language, encompasses the use, purpose, or function of speech and language in different contexts (Adams, 2005). Different functions of language include requesting, protesting, or commenting and can be communicated verbally or nonverbally. Nonverbal behaviors include facial expressions, gestures, and body proximity. Social Communication, the cognitive functions that support successful social interactions such as knowing another person's intent, understanding emotion, and making inferences in social interactions, is also an important aspect of Social Communication. Social Communication skills develop across communication developmental stages, including prelinguistic (i.e., before words are used) and emerging language stages (e.g., using single words and combining words) (ASHA, 2007b).

Social Communication begins within the first months, when infants look toward others' faces and specifically to their eyes. Eye contact helps the infant share the caregiver's focus of interest and leads to the development of many skills, including understanding of facial expressions, words, intentions, emotions, RJA, and IJA, all of which facilitate interaction with others (Hwa-Froelich, 2015; Senju & Csibra, 2008; Zhou, Chen, & Main, 2012). Eye gaze quickly expands to a variety of gestures such as reaching, pointing, or pulling toward an item and handing an item in order to get help, to open, or to activate. Gestures, one of the most consistent early indicators of early communicative intention (Crais, Douglas, & Campbell, 2004), can be classified into three types: those used for social interaction, those used to regulate others' behavior, and those used for joint attention (Bruner, 1981; Crais et al, 2004). Gestures used for social interaction include waving hi or bye or responding to "so big." Gestures that regulate behavior include pointing to ask for something out of reach, pushing away an undesired item, or shaking one's head to indicate "no." Gestures that result in joint attention direct another person's attention to something or someone, such as pointing to a dog outside or holding up a toy to share with another person (Bruner; Crais et al.). After a child uses gestures, vocalizations and word approximations develop as other means to communicate intentions and to interact with others. Table 8.1 illustrates the progression of early vocal skills and gestures, by function, that is seen in typical development.

Social Communication is one of the core deficits in ASD. In their review of the literature, Landa, Holman, O'Neil, and Stuart (2011) identified social and communicative challenges that distinguish ASD from typical development and developmental delay, including difficulty with initiation, reciprocal interaction, joint attention, symbolic behavior, motor imitation, understanding language, and gesture use. The impact of autism on Social Communication is seen early in development, and these impairments affect development of skills that establish and maintain engagement with communication partners, including parents, siblings, child care teachers, and peers. Very young children who have ASD have infrequent and short periods of interaction and engagement. This limits opportunities for language and social learning and necessitates targeted intervention. At 12 months, infants who later received an ASD diagnosis were found to have fewer gestures and to have less variety in gestures used to initiate social interaction when compared with typically developing infants (Colgan et al., 2006; Mitchell et al., 2006). The significant differences

Table 8.1.   Approximate developmental progression of early vocal skills and gestures by function

Function: Protest	Function: Request	Function: Social interaction/attention
Cries	Cries	
Arches body		
Vocalizes	Vocalizes	Vocalizes
Pushes away		
Moves away	Continues body movement such as bouncing after being bounced	
Shakes head no	Takes adult's hand on body to *continue* action	Waves in imitation
Says no	Reaches to be picked up	Waves when requested
	Initiates adult's hand on body to *begin* action	Spontaneously waves when others leave or enter
	Leads adult to desired object	Imitates Peekaboo or Pat-a-cake
	Reaches/points across a distance	Initiates Peekaboo or Pat-a-cake
	Points	Imitates clapping
	Gives to request help, open, or more	Initiates clapping
	Approximates word to request	Shows objects
	Says or nods yes to indicate a want	Gives objects
	Uses word to request	Points to show
	Uses phrase to request	Gestures in fingerplays and songs
		Fills in words in songs and rhymes
		Comments spontaneously
		Says or nods yes to indicate agreement

Sources: Crais, Douglas, and Campbell (2004); Crais, Watson, and Baranek (2009); Rosetti (2006).

between infants who have autism and those who have a developmental delay or who are developing typically in using joint attention gestures during the period of 12–24 months of age suggest that the absence of this Social Communication skill is often an early feature of autism (Watson, Crais, Baranek, Dykstra, & Wilson, 2013).

Speech differences are common in children with ASD as well as in infants at risk for ASD. In a study by Paul, Fuerst, Ramsay, Chawarska, and Klin (2011), infants at risk for ASD vocalized fewer consonant and consonant–vowel combinations and were noted to have more nonspeech sounds in early vocalizations than infants who were typically developing. These differences were related to the appearance of symptoms of autism in the second year. Other speech differences that may occur in ASD are speech errors and atypical stress or intonation of words or sentences. Some children with autism also receive a diagnosis of childhood apraxia of speech, a neurological disorder characterized by difficulties with the precision and consistency of the motor movements involved in speech when neuromuscular deficits such as abnormal reflexes or abnormal muscle tone are absent (ASHA, 2007b). The core impairment in planning and/or programming movements for speech sounds within and across words results in errors in speech sounds (e.g., using an incorrect sound, omitting a sound, saying a sound incorrectly), intonation, and stress of words and syllables. In a study of 46 children with ASD who were talking and whose speech was understandable, Shriberg, Paul, Black, and van Santen (2011) found a higher prevalence of delayed development of speech sounds and higher rates of speech errors when compared with typically developing youngsters. The children with ASD revised words, and their intonation was characterized by loud and/or high-pitched words and phrases and inappropriate syllable stress. Despite these errors, the children in the study did not have core features of childhood apraxia of speech.

According to Mody (2014), 25% of individuals with ASD do not develop functional speech. In her review of the literature, Mody found that the transition from nonverbal communication to primarily verbal means of communication occurs in the early years when children develop an awareness of the value of their communicative behaviors to give and receive messages between people. Less interest in the social world may interfere with the children's learning that actions have predictable meanings. As a result of decreased interest in the social world, children may, for example, exclusively attend to the object they are handling, unaware of and unmotivated by others' attempts to engage in social interactions, which has cascading ramifications for social and verbal learning.

Atypical language development also occurs in children with ASD. One aspect of this atypical development involves a discrepancy between use of language and understanding of language. A 17-year follow-up study with children who were evaluated for possible autism showed that expressive skills often exceeded receptive skills as language competence developed (Pickles, Anderson, & Lord, 2014). Better expressive than receptive skills can be confusing for EI providers and for families who assume that if a child uses a word, he or she comprehends its meaning. Another discrepancy sometimes seen in young children with ASD is the ability to label but not to request. For example, a child may see an object or a picture and may name it spontaneously but be unable to say the same word when asked "What's that?" or when the child wants the item. In addition, some children can answer when asked "What's that?" but cannot spontaneously request using the same word. Looking at the function of language from the perspective of verbal behavior can help EI providers discern a child's strengths and needs. Skinner (1957), using a behavioral framework to classify language development, identified six types of "verbal behaviors," four of which are relevant to infants and toddlers: mands, tacts, echoics, and intraverbals. Mands are requests and include asking for something using a point, a picture, or a word. Tacts are names or labels such as pointing to a dog and saying "dog." Intraverbals are responding to others' words, such as when answering questions or filling in the blanks when someone pauses (e.g., when a parent sings a song and waits for the child to fill in the last word in a phrase). Echoics are repetitions of words said.

Children with autism frequently repeat words they hear, including scripts from television shows, advertisements, and movies. This is known as *scripting* and is sometimes considered to be a form of echolalia. Echolalia, "the repetition, with similar intonation, of words or phrases that someone else has said" (Kim, Paul, Tager-Flusberg, & Lord, 2014, p. 242), is common in autism. Echolalia can be immediate or delayed and has been found to have many functions, including to serve as the answer "yes," to give an individual more processing time, to serve as a request, to serve as a turn in a verbal exchange, and to serve as a label (Prizant, 1983). Echolalia can occur along with fluent speech or can be the only verbal productions that an individual uses.

Scrolling is another atypical language feature that commonly occurs in children with ASD. Scrolling is characterized by the child giving a list of responses until he or she arrives at the correct response. For example, a child who is asked, "What does the dog say?" may scroll and say, "Moo, meow, woof." Usually the responses are related as the child searches for the correct answer. Scrolling often occurs when a child is prompt dependent and/or when the child has not truly learned what response is required in a given situation (Sundberg, 2008). Dylan, a 2-year-old child diagnosed with ASD, began to exhibit scrolling, necessitating that his EI team collaborate and problem-solve to help him respond more appropriately. Dylan used gestures, including reaching for or pulling others to what he wanted, pointing to a choice in a field of two, signing MORE, and performing actions in songs and fingerplays. Dylan's family wanted him to increase his verbal skills, so his team used strategies to encourage sound and word imitation as well as strategies to help him fill in words in familiar phrases and songs. In addition, his team worked on imitation across simple consonant–vowel words such as *eat, ball,* and *on.* Highly motivating activities and objects were used, and Dylan began to imitate words. The team was very pleased that Dylan was talking, but then, after about 5 weeks of responding appropriately with word approximations or words, Dylan began to scroll. When he was expected to use a word, instead of choosing the correct word, he began to scroll through a variety of words and gestures. For example, to obtain a cracker, Dylan would sign the word *cracker*; say "Go, eat, on"; repeat some of the words and the sign; and then cry. His tendency to scroll was observed throughout a variety of routines, which was frustrating and confusing for him and his family. His family was upset by his "loss" of skills. Dylan had learned the power of communication, but as his repertoire expanded, unless he knew a rote response or had prompts to imitate, he was unsure what to do or say in a given situation to get what he wanted. As Dylan moved to a more symbolic representation of his communication intention, emphasis had been put on talking rather than on strengthening his intention through the use of gestures and words. He had not practiced enough in a variety of routines using nonverbal problem solving and gestures such as handing over for help, taking a person to what he wanted, or pointing to what he wanted in combination with talking to build the necessary foundation. When the team changed its focus and targeted nonverbal problem solving and gesture use along with words, Dylan's scrolling disappeared.

EI providers have the challenge of analyzing activities and routines to tease out which skills are affecting interaction and looking at functional outcomes within family priorities. An EI provider's experiences with Sanjay and his family illustrate scenarios that are frequently encountered when working with young children with ASD. Sanjay was 2 years old and did not use any words or gestures when he began EI services. He made sounds when engaging in self-stimulatory behaviors such as rocking and spinning in circles. During the first session, Sanjay's parents expressed their priority: they wanted Sanjay to talk. The EI provider explained how foundation skills such as joint attention and gestures would support learning to talk. This confused Sanjay's parents: they did not understand why the EI provider did not begin teaching their intelligent son how to say words. As sessions progressed, the EI provider was able to help Sanjay's mother and father understand how fostering eye contact, attention, social interaction, problem-solving, and imitation laid the foundation so that Sanjay would be able to use gestures and words functionally. The EI provider helped Sanjay's parents learn to facilitate Sanjay's understanding of how he could affect the actions of others, first using prelinguistic skills and then through talking during their everyday routines.

When children are nonverbal or minimally verbal, augmentative and alternative modes of communication are often introduced. The Picture Exchange Communication System (PECS; Bondy & Frost, 1994) is an example of a popular program taught to young children who are not yet verbally communicating effectively. The PECS program entails a specific protocol and is not synonymous with using pictures to provide choices, though the latter can be a helpful strategy when working with individuals who are unable to verbalize requests consistently. Other alternative and augmentative communication options include sign language, applications for electronic tablets, and speech generating devices. At times, the need for an augmentative or alternative communication mode arises when a child is making a transition to a new setting such as a child care center or preschool class. This occurred when Misael began attending a preschool class for 2-year-olds. He was able to say words, phrases, and sentences at home with his parents, but his communication in other settings was limited. In preschool, he did not make comments to peers, make requests during play or snack time, or say the names of his classmates during a circle time activity, though his parents knew that he knew their names. At times, Misael said phrases that did not relate to what was happening, and when asked a question, he often repeated it rather than answering. During certain routines, such as when completing a puzzle, his speech was relevant, though not directed to others. For example, when completing an animal puzzle, he often said, "A cow says moo; a pig says oink," but he did not look to others nearby. Misael's team collaborated shortly after he began attending preschool and brainstormed about ways to use alternative and augmentative communication to help Misael interact more with his peers and teachers. They were able to allay Misael's parents' fears that using these strategies would prevent him from talking and discussed with them the short-term and long-term benefits of aided communication. Misael began to use pictures to make requests at snack time and photos of his classmates to participate at circle time, and after several weeks he no longer needed them. During sessions, his EI providers targeted peer interaction, and Misael's skills flourished.

EI providers typically use a developmental frame of reference to decide the next skills to target. This works well in many instances; however, because of the complexities of ASD, sometimes moving to the next step in a skill can uncover gaps in a child's development in a related area. For example, many times when a child has an expressive vocabulary of over 20 or so words, providers begin to target phrases. In some instances, if a child is not using single words for a variety of functions or if words tend to be imitated rather than spontaneous, the child may not be ready to expand his or her length of utterances. This was seen with Clarence, a 25-month-old child who had red flags for autism. Clarence's EI provider designed a board that on the left-hand side had a picture representing I WANT. On the right side were icons for four choices: TV, DRINK, EAT, and TICKLES. Because Clarence could not yet combine the words, his family and therapist began to help Clarence use one word at a time. Over time, the use of the board was faded; however, Clarence began every request by saying "I want" and did not specify what he wanted. In addition, he inappropriately began to use "I want" at the beginning of comments. He had mastered the goal of putting words together, but his phrases were not functional.

EI providers can help families and other caregivers to make a significant impact in their children's Social Communication and functional language. By embedding strategies into their daily routines, the following skills can be facilitated: looks into others' eyes; imitates gestures, sounds, and words; uses gestures for a variety of functions; uses words for a variety of functions; and participates in multiple exchanges with gestures and/or words. These skills are presented in the approximate order in which they occur developmentally and can be thought of as developmental milestones towards Social Communication.

Looks into Others' Eyes

Background Information: Eye contact supports the development of many early social-communicative skills, including joint attention, and is one of the first skills that establishes a foundation for Social Communication (Zhou et al., 2012). Eye contact is present in infants when they are sucking from the breast or bottle and when spoken to and is the stimulus that evokes a smile and facial recognition (Beier & Spelke, 2012). Social smiles are often shared within familiar, playful routines that families create. These playful routines include Peekaboo and tickle and chase games. They involve familiar, repetitive, and predictable movements and words that families have learned or have created.

Relevance to Children with Autism: Decreased eye contact is often present in individuals with ASD. Infants later diagnosed with autism show a decline in looking at others' eyes between ages 2 and 6 months, a finding not observed in typical development (Jones & Klin, 2013). Many children with autism do not consistently look at others when communicating, which affects their ability to receive important nonverbal information from the speaker and also may affect the other speaker's motivation to interact. In young children with ASD, playing sensory-social games is an effective way to evoke eye contact, as these routines teach children with ASD that eye contact results in something pleasurable and meaningful.

How to Incorporate into Routines: The following are ideas for practicing eye contact that may fit into a child's routine.

Bath Time/Dressing and Diapering

Play Peekaboo with a towel, a clean diaper, or the child's clothing. Use predictable language and sensory-social games the child likes, such as "I'm going to get your belly…." When dressing the child, position him or her so he or she can easily see your face.

Bedtime

Pause in the midst of the familiar bedtime routine of placing the child in the crib or tucking him or her in bed, wait for eye contact, and then smile and kiss the child goodnight.

Book Time

Position the child so he or she can easily look at you. Many times, book reading is done with the child in the reader's lap; however, other positions such as the child on a couch and the reader on the floor are more conducive to facilitating eye contact. When talking about the pictures or reading the book, establish a pattern using predictable words and sounds the child enjoys. As the routine becomes more familiar, pause, using expectant inflection so the child will look at you in anticipation of the next sound or word. Begin with one or two pauses, and as the child's eye contact improves, increase the expectations.

Community Outings

Playfully chase a child who is able to be safe while running or walking quickly, saying "I'm going to get you!" When sitting on a blanket at the park, play tickle or bouncing games, pausing to evoke eye contact. When the child is in a wagon or stroller, play "go and stop" games, using the words to gain smiles and anticipation. When waiting at the drive-through or in lines, play Peekaboo to engage the child. At the grocery store, hold items close to your face and talk about them before putting them in the cart.

Playtime

Use songs, rhymes, and finger plays enjoyed by the child, such as Peekaboo and Pat-a-cake. Sit the child in a box or laundry basket and sing "Row, Row, Row Your Boat."

Tips and Hints for Looking into Others' Eyes

Be aware of the child's sensory preferences to ensure the interactions are enjoyable (see Chapter 6).

When first targeting eye contact in daily routines and until the child demonstrates eye contact consistently, as much as possible limit distractions and position yourself and the child so it is easy for the child to look at your eyes.

The use of repetition of actions and language in all routines facilitates a child's understanding of the routine and sets the stage for the implementation of the strategy of pausing to evoke eye contact. Once a child knows the routine, an unexpected pause usually results in the child looking at the person to see why the word or action did not occur. This technique can be incorporated into any routine, such as when handing a child pieces of food, when singing a familiar song, when reading a familiar book, or when reciting a familiar fingerplay or rhyme. In addition, during interactions, the use of varying intonation, high affect, and expressions such as "wow" and "uh-oh" may help evoke eye contact.

When a child is engaged in activities that have repetition with multiple items (e.g., eating small crackers, playing with puzzles and blocks, putting objects into a container), be in control of the items the child needs and, for the first several, hand them to the child one at a time. After a few "freebies," pause so the child will look at you as if to say, "Where is the next one?" Once the child understands the expectation, he or she will look to request.

It is important to target eye contact as a Social Communication skill so the child learns that looking at someone's eyes has positive consequences such as gaining an item or information. Telling a child "Look at my eyes" or "Look at me" targets following directions rather than evoking spontaneous eye contact at appropriate times.

Turning and looking at the speaker when one's name is called is related to looking at others' eyes. Teaching a child to turn to his or her name can be accomplished by calling the child's name when handing him or her desired items and when giving positive comments. If the child understands language associated with enjoyable activities (e.g., "Time to go outside," "Let's go bye-bye"), call his or her name before using the familiar phrase. The child will associate turning to his or her name with positive consequences. In some instances, especially if a child has challenging behavior, the child hears his or her name under circumstances that decrease the likelihood of turning to his or her name. For example, during a team meeting, the EI provider helped Bobbie's parents and child care teachers realize that they used his name much more frequently when making statements such as "Bobbie, get down," "Bobbie, stop that," and "Bobbie, take that out of your mouth" than when they gave him positive comments such as "Good listening."

Looking toward where someone is pointing is a skill that is beneficial to target once a child consistently uses eye contact. This important Social Communication skill is a component of RJA. To teach a child to follow a point, begin by sitting or standing near a bowl containing favorite snacks that is out of reach of the child but within view. Say "Look!" using an excited tone of voice as you point to the snack. If the child does not look, tap the bowl and/or wiggle it to help draw the child's attention to it. As soon as the child looks at the bowl, give him or her one snack item. Repeat this process and fade the cues of tapping and/or waving the bowl. In addition, as the child gains the skill of following a point to a close object, move farther from the bowl so the distance between the pointing finger and the target increases. Generalize the skill by pointing to a variety of items that match the child's interests and preferences that are varying distances away.

Ideas for Monitoring Progress: Note the number of time the child looks at another's eyes during a 3-minute interval during specific routines and/or the number of times the child turns to his or her name and looks at the speaker's eyes in a given number of opportunities.

Imitates Gestures, Sounds, and Words

Background Information: Imitation of gestures, sounds, and words is an important component of both social and cognitive development. Children begin to imitate gestures within family routines, such as when waving hi and bye and blowing kisses; when performing actions to rhymes and songs such as "Pat-a-cake," "The Itsy Bitsy Spider," and "The Wheels on the Bus"; and when engaging in pretend play activities such as when holding a hand up to the ear to pretend to talk on the phone. Imitation of sounds begins in vocal play and progresses to imitation of environmental and animal sounds and then words.

Relevance to Children with Autism: Individuals with ASD imitate less frequently and less accurately from infancy on and continue to show impairments throughout the life span. Challenges are more significant when imitation requires copying actions and goals without knowledge of the end product or the function of the materials used (Vivanti & Hamilton, 2014). Children with ASD, both verbal and nonverbal, who do not readily use gestures benefit from imitation activities to help them learn to problem-solve using their bodies. Examples include gently pushing others to move them out of the way, handing to others for help, holding out a limb for dressing activities, and answering questions such as "What should I do?" when the answer needed is an action. These gestures help children learn the power of communication and lay the foundation for more abstract gesture use. Helpful gestures to model and target for imitation include come, I want, my turn, head nods, and head shakes.

How to Incorporate into Routines: The following are ideas for practicing gestures, sounds, and words that may fit into a child's routine.

Bath Time

Model actions such as splashing water and blowing suds. When playing with tub toys, model actions such as making the fish swim, sounds such as "b-b-b-b" for a boat, and words such as "quack-quack" for a duck. Wave and say "hi" and "bye" to toys when putting them in the tub and when putting them away. At the end of bath time, say and gesture "all done" and help the child imitate the gesture if he or she does not say the words or imitate the gesture.

Bedtime

Pat the child's stuffed animals and tell them "Night-night." Help the child to do the same. Put your fingers to your lips and say "Shhh" or "Night-night" to the child. Once the child can imitate, model saying goodnight to the stuffed animals.

Book Time

Use gestures to represent actions and concepts in the pictures. For example, use gestures to represent up, down, big, round and round, sleeping, eating, and jumping. Pretend to take a cupcake from a picture of a birthday party and "eat" the cupcake, or blow on a picture of hot food and then encourage the child, "Your turn! You do it too!" Model making sounds and saying words that correspond to the pictures such as "Mmm!" and "Eat" for pictures of food.

Community Outings

At the park, repeatedly place a toy car, a ball, or stones on the slide and model "Whee!" as the objects roll down. Hand the child the items and, if needed, help him or her place them on the slide. As you approach the automatic doors at the grocery store, library, or post office, say "open" and model signing OPEN. If the child does not say the word, assist him or her to make the sign.

Diapering and Dressing

When taking off the child's shirt, say "So big!" and model up-stretched arms. Help the child imitate arms up. After diapering, hold out your hands and say "Up." If the child does not reach, tap his or her hands and hold your hands very close to the child's in hopes he or she will reach for them. Over time, hold your hands farther away so the child will stretch farther and farther, turning a reach for your hands into the gesture for "up."

Grooming and Hygiene

Brushing teeth, brushing hair, washing hands, and washing the face provide many opportunities for imitation due to the presence of objects that help cue the child as to the purpose of the activity as well the needed motor movements. Model the actions needed while saying important key words such as "Brush-brush-brush" or "Rub-rub-rub."

Household Activities

Tell the child what you will be doing and model any appropriate corresponding environmental sounds, actions, and words. For example, when getting ready to vacuum, say to the child, "Time to vacuum," make the whirring sound of a vacuum, and pretend to push a vacuum back and forth before turning on the vacuum.

Mealtime/Snack Time

Make playful faces, such as sticking out your tongue or smacking your lips. Use sounds and words to describe the food such as "Mmm," "Yummy," "Hot," or "Eat." When preparing and cleaning up after meals, provide opportunities for the child to imitate stirring, tearing lettuce, rinsing plastic dishes, and wiping off the highchair tray or table. Model the movements of the activity and corresponding words.

Playtime

Model actions and their corresponding sounds and words such as shaking, pushing, flying, banging, filling, dumping, and sweeping, beginning with actions that are within both the child's play and motor repertoires and progressing to novel ones. Examples include rolling a toy car and saying "Vroom" or "Beep-beep," placing a small blanket or towel on a stuffed animal and with your finger on your lips saying "Shhh. Night-night," and knocking on the wall saying "Knock, knock." When something unexpected happens, such as when a block tower falls or a ball rolls behind the sofa, say "Oh, man." Many children, over time, will begin to repeat the phrase. Similarly, when a child successfully places a piece in a puzzle or a pom-pom in a bottle, exclaim "Ta-da!", as many children will imitate the intonation or the sounds. As the child's imitation and play skills improve, incorporate novel sounds and words into more advanced play schemes such as pretending to carry a purse or backpack and leaving to go to the store, work, or school. If it is difficult to join a child in play to model actions and words (e.g., if the child moves away when approached), begin by observing the child from a distance and on occasion comment about what the child is doing and imitate the child's sounds and actions. Gradually move closer, and once the proximity is tolerated, imitate the child's actions and sounds. When the child tolerates side-by-side proximity with imitated models, gain the child's trust by occasionally imitating the child and/or handing him or her items related to the play. Gradually increase the frequency of interactions, and when well tolerated, begin to target imitation.

Tips and Hints for Imitating Gestures, Sounds, and Words

When interacting with the child throughout all routines, use gestures to augment spoken language. Playfully exaggerate actions such as running, walking, and marching as well as feelings such as being cold (i.e., shivering and saying "Brrr").

Modeling a gesture along with speech allows for opportunities to imitate actions, sounds, and/or words. Some children with ASD imitate gestures more easily than speech, whereas others more easily imitate speech than gestures, depending on their strengths and needs as well as their developmental level. When first targeting imitation of gestures, sounds, and/or words, take notice of trends that reveal whether the child is better able to imitate gesturally or verbally in order to plan strategies to progress from easier to more challenging demands.

For early learners, use consistent actions and simplified language (e.g., "Time to wash hands" rather than "Let's go into the bathroom and wash your hands") in order to increase understanding of language and to provide easier models to imitate.

Develop a repertoire of songs, rhymes, and fingerplays to incorporate into routines to help make the activity fun, predictable, and more easily imitated (e.g., sing "This Is the Way We Wash Our Hands" and "This Is the Way We Put on Our Shoes").

Model gestures such as one to mean "all done" across routines (e.g., when a child is finished with a meal or snack, when the child's diaper changing is finished, when the child's nose is wiped).

At first, many children need physical assistance to imitate gestures. Some children more readily accept hand-under-hand than hand-over-hand help. In addition, when using physical prompts to help with imitation, it is often necessary to systematically fade the assistance. For example, if helping a child sign OPEN, begin by helping the child with the complete gesture. Over time, put the child's hands together and then wait for the child to move them apart. When the child independently moves his or her hands apart, hold his or her hands but wait to see if the child moves his or her hands together. If so, after several instances of success, pause to see if the child completes the motor movements. If not, provide the least amount of assistance needed.

To facilitate attention and motivation to imitate, use high affect, silliness, and activities the child finds fun.

When available, use other children or adults as models so the child sees others imitating the targeted gesture, sound, or word.

Following a developmental trajectory of imitation skills will help match the task to the child's level, ensuring an appropriate target. For example, if a child is unable to imitate sounds and words, imitation of two-word phrases should not be targeted.

Use repetition and slow movement when modeling a new gesture in order to give the child time to process.

When encouraging gesture use and verbal skills simultaneously, it is sometimes difficult to discern whether the child is imitating the action or following the verbal direction. For example, Sarah's mother said "Clap" as she clapped her hands and then Sarah clapped. The EI provider was unsure if Sarah was responding to her mother's direction or her mother's clapping. To determine this, the EI provider suggested that Sarah's mother first clap her hands without saying the word. Sarah did not respond. Sarah's mother then said "Clap," and Sarah clapped her hands. They both knew that Sarah was following the direction but not imitating.

Ideas for Monitoring Progress: Make a list of the gestures, sounds, or words the child is imitating within specific routines and/or ways imitation has increased participation in routines.

Uses Gestures for a Variety of Functions

Background Information: Children use a variety of gestures for various purposes, including to protest, to request actions, to request objects, to seek attention, to play social games, to comment, to request information, and to represent emotions and ideas (Crais et al., 2004). In typical development, gestures begin to develop before speech; however, gestures continue to augment verbal communication throughout the life span (Goldin-Meadow & Alibali, 2013). In the later parts of their first year and through their second year, young children generalize gestures learned during interactive routines to new situations. For example, a child may see a spider outside, look toward a parent, and put his or her hands together to form a spider, just like when they sing "The Itsy Bitsy Spider." At this age, children also use gestures such as head shaking for "no" and head nodding for "yes" as well as actions such as bouncing to indicate the desire to be bounced while sitting on a parent's knees (Goodwyn, Acredolo, & Brown, 2000).

Relevance to Children with Autism: Infants with autism have been found to use fewer gestures and fewer types of gestures when compared with infants who are developing typically as well as when compared with those who have other developmental disabilities (Colgan et al., 2006; Mitchell et al., 2006; Watson et al., 2013). According to Goodwyn et al. (2000), encouraging gesture use in young children may lead to more rapid language development. Facilitating gesture use during daily routines has yielded positive results when working with infants and toddlers with ASD and related disorders, as many young children have learned the power of communication through these activities.

How to Incorporate into Routines: The following are ideas for practicing using gestures for a variety of functions that may fit into a child's routine.

Bath Time

Hold out your hands to encourage the child to lift his or her hands to be helped in and out of the tub. When the child consistently reaches up, wait without putting your hands out to see if the child lifts his or her hands to indicate he or she is ready to get in or out. If the child does not lift his or her arms, ask "Are you ready to get out?" and if the child does not gesture, once again give the visual cue of outstretched hands. To facilitate a reach/point to request, hold out two bath toys and ask which one the child wants.

Bedtime

Use the same strategies as in Bath Time to teach a child how to reach to indicate help getting in and out of the crib or bed.

Book Time

Hold out two books for the child to choose from by reaching or pointing. Tell the child to show you actions in books such as the wheels turning, the rabbit hopping, or the squirrel running up the tree. Model them if necessary and fade the models over time.

Community Outings

Pause before putting the child into his or her car seat, waiting for the child to lift his or her arms to be picked up. At the store, hold up items for the child to choose, such as green apples or red apples.

Dressing and Diapering

Use the strategies discussed in the Bath Time section to encourage the child to reach up to get on and off the changing table. When dressing the child, playfully put a sock on the child's hand and wait for a response. If the child does not react, say "That doesn't go on your hand! Where does that go?" Tap the child's foot if he or she does not move it or point to it. Pretend to put on the child's clothing and playfully say, "No, that's not mine. Whose _____ is this?" to encourage the child to show ownership with a gesture such as trying to put on the item or pointing to himself or herself.

Grooming and Hygiene

For established routines, ask the child "What do we do next?" For example, while holding the child's toothbrush, ask "Now what do you do?" to encourage the child to show you with a hand motion that toothbrushing is next.

Mealtime/Snack Time

Place desired food items out of reach so the child will need to pull you to get them and/or reach or point to show you what he or she wants. Give the child small portions of food and drink so he or she will need to ask for more by handing over the dish or cup or by pointing.

Playtime

Place some desired toys out of reach to encourage reaching or pointing to request. Embed gestures into pretend play such as those to represent sleeping, eating, and drinking.

Tips and Hints for Using Gestures for a Variety of Functions

Handing an item to another person to request help is a valuable early gesture to target. Many parents remark that their children are independent and never ask for help, but in the authors' experience, this is often because the children do not know how to ask for help. Communication temptations to use include blowing bubbles several times and then putting the lid tightly on the jar of bubbles, placing snack foods in clear containers, and winding up small toys, leaving the items in front of the child to hand over to request help, more, or open. If the child does not pick up the item and hand it over, hold out your hand and ask, "Do you want _____?" Some children may need another person to sit or stand behind them to help them hand over the item. This assistance needs to be faded quickly or the child may not gain independence.

For children who scream, cry, hit, or bite to gain attention, teaching them to use a replacement gesture can significantly reduce unwanted behaviors. A beneficial strategy for teaching a child how to appropriately gain attention is to help the child gently tap a parent's arm or leg and for the parent to playfully respond with an exaggerated "Hi" or an expectant "Yes?" as soon as the child touches him or her. Multiple repetitions in a short period of time can be practiced if the parent pretends to be asleep or pretends to be reading. The skill can later be practiced and generalized in a variety of settings and situations. Other gestures such as waving or giving high-fives or fist bumps can also be taught to gain attention. For example, every day Jonah bit his peers at his child care center, and it was determined that he was doing so as a way to interact. His peers had begun to move away whenever he approached, as they did not want to get bitten. Jonah's EI provider taught him to approach his peers to give high-fives at the same time she helped his peers to respond to his gestures. Jonah learned he got attention, and the peers discovered Jonah did not bite them when they gave him the high-fives. After several weeks, his biting disappeared.

The sign for "open" is another functional gesture to target early. Initially, provide physical assistance by taking the child's hands to form the sign and fade the help as quickly as possible. Help the child use the sign in a variety of situations such as to request the opening of doors, containers, and books.

Teaching a child to reach and point to request opens the door for more communication and helps immensely with regulation. Some children overgeneralize the first gesture they learn and it becomes a universal way to indicate "I want." This can cause frustration for the child and for others. For example, Tara learned to indicate "open" by gesture and knew her needs were met when she got to the door, when she handed her mother some candy, and when she handed her bubbles. When she began to say "open" when pointing to her cup on the shelf and when handing her mother a toy for help, her mother and her EI provider realized that to Tara, *open* meant her needs would be met. Because this overgeneralization occurs frequently, it is strongly recommended that requesting with a reach/point be targeted before introducing a gesture for "more" or "open." As illustrated in Figure 8.1a and 8.1b, a good place to teach a child the power of his or her reaching to request is when seated in a highchair or booster seat, such as during a snack. Begin by handing the child one small snack item. When the child finishes eating that one, move your hand a little farther away. As soon as the child reaches, hand him or her the piece of food. Gradually move farther away, and as soon as the child's hand reaches, instantly bring the snack to the child's hand to grasp. The timing in this beginning stage is critical, as the child must receive the food as soon as his or hand goes out. As you gradually move back, if the child does not readily reach, move a little closer until the child reaches and after giving him or her the item, once again begin the process of moving farther away. Many children learn to reach to request across a distance in a short amount of time. Once the child is able to reach while seated in a highchair or elsewhere where he or she cannot move to grab the item, practice in settings where the child is not confined (see Figure 8.1c–8.1e). A similar method using a light switch on a wall also works well for children who like to turn lights on and off and is illustrated in Figure 8.1f–8.1h. Hold the child at the light switch and allow him or her to turn on and off the light. Move a short distance away from the light switch, and as the child reaches to turn it on or off, quickly move so the child

Figure 8.1a

Figure 8.1b

Figure 8.1c

Figure 8.1d

Figure 8.1. These photos depict strategies to teach a child to reach and point to request. The photos in Figure 8.1a and 8.1b show the child seated in his high-chair, reaching to request a snack. Most children need to be held or confined in a highchair or booster during the initial phases to prevent them from moving to grab the desired items. In Figure 8.1a, the early intervention (EI) provider is demonstrating how to hold a piece of food close to the child, giving him the treat as soon as he reaches so he begins to associate his outstretched hand with communicating his desire to obtain what he sees. In Figure 8.1b, the EI provider is demonstrating how to move a little farther away from the child to present the food. As soon as his arm was extended, she moved toward him to give him the food. Figure 8.1c shows the child's mother practicing with her son. He reached to indicate he wanted the snack, and as soon as he did, she gave him one piece. Figure 8.1d shows the child has learned to point with his index finger, communicating across a short distance. In Figure 8.1e, the child points across the room to indicate he wants another treat. The photos in Figure 8.1f–8.1h show a similar method to teach a child to reach or point to request using a wall light switch. The child's mother held him at the light switch and allowed him to turn the lights on and off several times. She then moved a short distance away from the light switch, and as soon as he extended his arm, she moved him to the switch so he could turn on the light. She repeated this several times, each time moving a little farther away until he was pointing to indicate he wanted to flip the switch.

Figure 8.1e

Figure 8.1f

Figure 8.1g

Figure 8.1h

is successful. Gradually move farther and farther away, quickly moving to the light switch as soon as the child's hand reaches toward the switch. When initially teaching this skill, set up situations that ensure many repetitions within a short amount of time such as the light switch and the snack afford. Practice then can be gleaned from other routines such as when handing the child desired items like his or her bottle, cup, and toys.

It is important to ensure generalization of gestures across people, places, and objects. For example, encourage a child to wave "bye-bye" to his father as he goes to work, to the dog that is walking by, and to his or her cousin who is at the park. In the authors' experiences, if gestures are not practiced in a variety of functional contexts, the child may stop using them before having another way to communicate.

It is important to analyze under what conditions a child uses gestures and to expand the repertoire of situations. For example, a child may point to answer a question but not to spontaneously show something to another person. Similarly, a child may point to request but not to answer a question. Some children use gestures in familiar routines such as in songs but do not generalize to other situations to show, request, or answer a question.

Ideas for Monitoring Progress: List the gestures the child uses by function (see Table 8.1), the prompt level the child needs to use a gesture, and/or how gestures enable the child to participate in a specific routine.

Uses Words for a Variety of Functions

Background Information: As with gestures, words are used for a wide variety of purposes: to protest, to request attention, to request items, to request actions, to comment, to answer questions, and to ask questions. Children begin with word approximations and then progress to using single words and then word combinations.

Relevance to Children with Autism: Among individuals with autism, there is a wide variety of verbal abilities. Some individuals are nonverbal, whereas others have extensive vocabularies; however, the functional use of language (pragmatics) is a universal challenge for those with ASD (Miniscalco, Rudling, Råstam, Gillberg, & Johnels, 2014). Some children can name colors, shapes, and numbers but do not use words interactively. Children with ASD often have challenges using words in specific situations. For example, a child may have a vocabulary of many words and phrases but may be unable to use the same words to request or answer a question, even after a model to imitate. This often leads to frustration for the child and for those who care for him or her. Parents often remark "I know he can say that" and may think that the child is being stubborn when the child has not yet learned how to use language for different functions.

How to Incorporate into Routines: The following are ideas for practicing using words for a variety of functions that may fit into a child's routine.

Bath Time

To facilitate requesting, set up situations so desired items for the bath are outside the child's reach. Vary word models to target requesting and commenting (e.g., when the child wants the duck, say, "You want the duck. Say 'duck,'" and after the child has the duck, say, "You have the duck. Say 'duck.'").

Bedtime

Set up the situation to encourage the child to use a variety of words such as to request a stuffed animal on the shelf, to request being picked up, to name which book to read, and to make a choice about which pajamas he or she wants to wear.

Book Time

Give the child choices of books to read. For some pictures, model comments, and for others, ask the child questions that are appropriate for his or her level of language comprehension. For example, begin with "What's that?" and "Who's that?" to target nouns, and when those are mastered, progress to "What is he doing?" to target actions with –ing endings. For children who can answer these types of questions, ask about the function of objects such as "Show me something we eat with."

Community Outings

Set up opportunities for the child to make requests, such as "up" to get in the car, "out" to get out of the shopping cart, "more" to be pushed again on the swing, or "jump" to obtain help to jump over cracks in the sidewalk. As you explore in the community, comment about what you see. As the child's language skills develop, ask what he or she sees.

Dressing and Diapering

Give choices of where the child wants a diaper change and what clothes to wear. Make comments about the color of the clothing and any depicted animals or objects on the clothes, and for children who can answer, ask questions such as "What do we need to put on your feet?" or "What do we put on next?"

Grooming and Hygiene

When brushing the child's hair or teeth, sing a song and pause for the child to fill in words, such as "This is the way we brush your _____." Ask "Now what?" when the child knows what comes next in the sequence.

Household Activities

Ask the child if he or she wants to help with household activities such as watering plants or rinsing dishes. When the child is helping, make comments about what he or she is doing and ask relevant questions.

Mealtime/Snack Time

Give choices of food and drink for the child to select. Playfully sabotage situations such as giving ice cream, applesauce, or another scoopable food but not a spoon to a child who typically uses a spoon. If the child does not request a spoon, ask the child "What do you need?" Give the child small portions so he or she must ask for more. Comment about the taste, smell, temperature, and color of foods.

Tips and Hints for Using Words for a Variety of Functions

Model words that correspond to the child's gestures and word approximations.

Functional communication may include gestures, pictures, and/or words. A child who has a repertoire of spontaneous gestures and/or pictures used for a variety of functions is able to communicate more effectively than a child who is verbal but only labels or who talks only when prompted. If a child is verbal but does not use his or her words in a variety of ways, consider strengthening the child's use of gestures and/or pictures.

Some children with ASD more easily comment than request, especially when they are dysregulated. To help a child learn that the same word can be a comment and a request, model the different uses of the word. For example, when the child asks for a cookie, comment "Mmm! Cookie! Cookie. You are eating a cookie."

To help a child learn to call for a parent instead of crying or tugging on a hand or clothing, have the parent hide just out of sight. Another person (e.g., a sibling, the EI provider) then calls for the parent, who playfully appears and responds with an exaggerated "Hi!" or an expectant "Yes?" Repeat several times and then, when the parent is hiding, pause to see if the child makes a sound or approximates calling for the parent. If the child does not respond, continue to provide the model. Practice in a variety of settings so the child learns to call in situations such as to get out of the crib or to get needed help.

Some children can answer the question "What is it?" but not "What do you want?" when the answer is the same word. Look for patterns of responses related to their function as well as prompts that are needed to help expand the child's pragmatic skills.

For children who can imitate words and who reach or point to request rather than using words spontaneously, use prompts such as "Good job showing me. Now use your mouth to tell me _____."

When gestures or words are overgeneralized, model a more appropriate response. For example, if the child calls everything that is round a circle, when he or she says "circle" to refer to a wheel, doughnut, or ball, model the name of the object. If the child overgeneralizes a gesture or word such as *up* or *more* to mean any request, model the correct gesture and/or word.

If a child says a word (e.g., "open," "more") only when he or she hears the word, the child may be imitating but not comprehending the meaning of the word. In children with ASD, receptive language skills must be assessed on an ongoing basis. It is common for children who have been working on imitation skills without a lot of work on receptive language skills and/or listening skills to repeat what they hear without carefully listening to the speaker. For example, Eduardo's team was targeting imitation, and when he was able to imitate speech well, whenever he was asked a question, he automatically repeated the last word, thinking that was the response others were seeking. His team began to target following directions and giving him choices with the first option being his preference to help him develop better listening skills.

Ideas for Monitoring Progress: Make lists of the words, their function, and in what routines they are used.

Participates in Multiple Exchanges with Gestures and/or Words

Background Information: Young infants participate in back and forth turn-taking with sounds and then discover that gestures such as moving back and forth when in the swing results in more swinging. These interactions expand, and children learn to engage in short "conversations" using gestures and words, resulting in skills such as relating experiences, answering and asking questions, and interjecting comments.

Relevance to Children with Autism: Conversation skills in children with ASD are often lacking. Responses tend to be short, initiations are sporadic, and there is little sharing of new and pertinent information, all of which affect social interaction (Koegel, Park, & Koegel, 2014). Though most children with ASD do not reach the conversation stage before making the transition to preschool, the following strategies can lay a foundation for expanding the number of exchanges during daily routines.

How to Incorporate into Routines: The following are ideas for practicing participating in multiple exchanges that may fit into a child's routine.

Bath Time

Ask questions such as "What should we wash now?" Over time, encourage the child to plan ahead by asking "And then what should we wash?" immediately after the child responds verbally or by pointing.

Bedtime

During the bedtime routine, talk about events of the day that were fun for the child. Ask relevant questions and comment about the child's statements.

Book Time

Take turns describing pictures. In familiar books, take turns talking about what happened on a particular page. For children who are not yet using many words, give choices of gestures. For example, ask, "Is the baby sleeping or eating?" and model gestures for sleeping and eating if needed.

Community Outings

When riding in the car, take turns saying "I see a _____." In the grocery store, expand on the child's comments and requests. For example, if the child asks for cookies, say, "Cookies taste good. What other foods do you like?" After the child responds, tell him or her foods that you like.

Dressing and Diapering

During dressing, lay an article of clothing next to the child. Hold out your hand to encourage the child to give you the item while telling the child "Give me your _____." When this becomes a familiar routine, place two items of clothing next to the child with the expectation that the child will give first one item and, after that item is on the child, he or she will give the second. Expand the child's responses by asking him or her "Where does this go?" and wait for the child to indicate nonverbally or verbally. Over time, the child will learn the sequence of dressing and will be participating by communicating.

Grooming and Hygiene

For children who know the sequence of brushing their teeth, pause at various places for the child to indicate what comes next. Narrate their actions, such as "Oh, you need toothpaste!"

Household Activities

Make a statement and ask a relevant question. For example, say, "The plants are thirsty. What do we need to do?" Another option is to ask sequences of related questions. For instance, when wiping the table, ask the child, "Where should I wipe first?"; after wiping that spot, ask, "Now where?"

Mealtime/Snack Time

Provide choices and ask questions related to the food and food preparation. Comment about the child's responses and make a related response. To encourage turn-taking and problem solving, use playful sabotage. For example, if a child asks for a drink of milk, get out the milk and wait for the child to indicate the need for a cup. Pretend to pour the unopened milk to see if the child indicates the need for the container to be opened. Affirm the child's communication by commenting on nonverbal responses and repeating or rephrasing verbal ones.

Playtime

Take turns with the child with objects such as rolling a ball back and forth, building with blocks, popping bubbles on a wand, and placing straws in a bottle, commenting about what you are doing when it is your turn. This may help the child understand that turn-taking happens with objects as well as with language. Sing familiar songs and pause for the child to fill in the appropriate word. Gradually increase the number of pauses to facilitate turn-taking.

Tips and Hints for Participating in Multiple Exchanges with Gestures and/or Words

Make relevant comments in response to the child's comments. For example, if a child labels "car," respond by saying, "My car is red" or "We rode in the car to go to the store." Ask questions such as "Where did Daddy go in the car?" or "Where is your car?" to keep the conversation going.

Ideas for Monitoring Progress: Record the number of back and forth turns the child demonstrates within a certain amount of time or during a specific routine.

PUTTING IT TOGETHER

As seen in this chapter, children with ASD exhibit a variety of Social Communication challenges that necessitate careful analysis by EI providers. Table 8.2 presents some of the common challenges and provides reasons they may occur as well as ideas for their remediation.

Table 8.2. Common communication challenges observed in young children with autism spectrum disorder

Problem	Features	Causes to consider	Hints to try from this and other chapters (as noted) in this book	Chapters from Crawford and Weber (2014) that may be helpful
Overgeneralizes	The child requests only by using the same sign, word, or phrase, such as "more," "open," "please," or "I want" in all situations. The child uses the same phrase over and over, such as "I want please."	The gesture, word, or phrase results in obtaining what is desired, reinforcing its use. The child may not have other options that are effective for him or her. The child may not have a large enough spontaneous vocabulary to request at the single-word level.	If the child does not point to request, target pointing.[a] Once a child points to request, target several words that will be relatively easy for the child to say and that will result in the child obtaining what is wanted. Avoid emphasizing word combinations until the child spontaneously requests using many different single words.	Chapter 6
Expressive language exceeds receptive language	The child uses gestures or words but does not demonstrate understanding of the same words.	The child does not have a core receptive vocabulary. The child may not have experience of following directions and tuning into language.	Target receptive vocabulary words that are functional, such as names of family members and common objects. Find opportunities for repetition and practice. Target one-step directions that are functional, are associated with positive experiences, and can be physically prompted, such as "Give me cup" and "Give me five" (See Chapter 6.)	Chapter 5
Does not follow directions	The child cooperates with following directions when helped to do so. The child refuses to follow directions.	The child may not be shifting attention to process the language. The child may need positive behavior strategies to build cooperation.	Practice shifting attention to sounds and words. Target receptive vocabulary as above. (See Chapter 6.) (See Chapters 3, 5, and 6.)	Chapter 5 Appendix A
Labels but does not request	The child names objects and/or pictures but does not use the same words to request.	The child has not learned the power of language using gestures and/or words. The child understands words but is unable to retrieve them when needed in order to request.	Turn the label into a request. For example, if the child sees a toy dog and says "dog" to label, hand the child the toy. Provide models for the child to imitate, and fade them as quickly as possible. (See Chapter 3.)	Chapter 6
Does not answer questions	The child does not respond to questions. The child repeats the last word or words instead of answering the question (e.g., "Do you want juice?" "Want juice."). The child always chooses the second choice from two options.	The child does not process/understand the question due to the complexity of the language. The child does not yet have a way to indicate yes. The child has overgeneralized the skill of imitating and/or is not yet able to comprehend two units of information.	Target listening skills and following directions. Target pointing to request if the child does not do so. If the child is able to point to request, target head nodding for yes. If the child does not gesture or say "no," this likely will need to be targeted first. Offer preferred items as the first option (e.g., "Do you want [favorite food] or [disliked food]?"), and if the child chooses the second option, give it to him or her. When he or she rejects the food, repeat the question, emphasizing the first choice.	Chapter 5 Chapter 5, Chapter 6
Prompt dependence	The child signs or says "All done" only if someone asks "All done?," waves good-bye only if someone says "Say bye-bye," and/or waits until someone asks "What do you want?" to request verbally or nonverbally.	The child attends to the prompt or follows a direction rather than makes an association between the situation and the response.	Systematically fade prompts. Target initiation using gestures and then words by setting up the environment using communication temptations. (See Chapter 3.)	Chapter 6

[a]Pointing in this chapter refers to the use of the index finger to communicate rather than the fine motor skill of index finger isolation. In some instances, children have the communicative intent to gesturally indicate a choice or to direct others to look but use their whole hand rather than their index finger. This also can be considered a communicative "point."

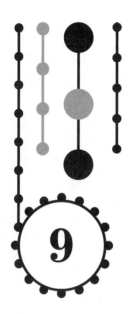

9

Daily Routines and Common Challenges

The recipe for success for an EI provider necessitates the combination of four ingredients: knowledge about EI, knowledge about development, knowledge about the child's family and their routines, and knowledge about teaching strategies and principles of learning. Those four ingredients are the basis for the book *Early Intervention Every Day!* (Crawford & Weber, 2014). For EI providers who work with young children who have a diagnosis of or symptoms of ASD, another ingredient is needed: knowledge of the relationship among Regulation; Making Sense of Self, Others, and the Environment; Flexibility; and Social Communication. The previous chapters in this book captured those ingredients; however, because each child and family is unique, there is no "cookbook" that can offer EI providers exact instructions when working with children with ASD and related disorders. This book was written to give EI providers the tools to problem-solve with parents and other caregivers in order to effectively target the learning and behavior challenges characteristic of young children who have autism or related disorders. The purpose of this chapter is to integrate information from the previous chapters and to highlight specific challenges that families face.

Many parents of young children with ASD report concerns regarding challenging behaviors. In a study of nearly 300 infants and toddlers, aggressive, destructive, self-injurious, and stereotypic behaviors were found to be present as early as 12 months of age and tended to increase to problematic levels between ages 25–39 months (Fodstad et al., 2012). Many families ask EI providers to help them manage these types of behaviors, and even when they do not, EI providers often find that these behaviors must be addressed in order to make progress on IFSP outcomes.

CASE STUDY ADDRESSING A FAMILY'S CONCERNS

The importance of addressing behaviors in order to make progress can be seen in the example of Ezekial, a 30-month-old toddler who had been adopted by his great aunt, Latoya. Latoya and the evaluators developed IFSP outcomes for Ezekial to use gestures and words to express his wants and needs, to increase the variety of foods eaten, and to sleep through the night. Because he hit or threw objects when he did not get what he wanted, when new foods were put on his plate, and when his aunt put him in his crib rather than in her bed, the team carefully devised strategies to decrease unwanted behaviors and to teach him new skills.

Ezekial's team consisted of a special instructor, an occupational therapist, and a speech-language pathologist. The team assessed the function of Ezekial's behavior and further explored factors related to his Regulation; his ability to Make Sense of Self, Others, and the Environment; his Flexibility; and his Social Communication. During the first few weeks of services, Latoya began to discuss her concerns about Ezekial's tantrums and running away when they were in the community as well as other behaviors including toe walking, hand flapping, and feces smearing. She was planning to take Ezekial and her granddaughter on a trip to Disney World, but she did not know how she was going to manage the airplane trip, Ezekial's selective eating, and the stress for all three of them when he had tantrums. She was afraid they might be removed from the airplane, but she had been promising her granddaughter this trip for several years.

Latoya's feelings and concerns are common among parents and caregivers. Stereotypies such as toe walking and hand flapping cause embarrassment for some parents. Toe walking in children with ASD has been associated with a persistent primitive reflex (Accardo & Barrow, 2015), and children with autism have been noted to have hypotonia, or low muscle tone, but it is unknown if this is a factor in toe walking (Shetreat-Klein, Shinnar, & Rapin, 2014). In the authors' (Crawford's and Weber's) experience, some children have been noted to toe walk more when barefoot, whereas others toe walk more when wearing shoes. Some children have been noted to walk on their toes more on certain surfaces than on others. Ezekial, for example, toe walked when on the grass but not on the sidewalk. In the house, when barefoot, he walked on his toes when on the carpet more than when he was on bare floors. Although toe walking is common in autism, it also occurs in other disorders (Accardo, Monasterio, & Oswald, 2014). Because of this, Ezekial's team requested a physical therapy consultation to determine if Ezekial was in need of any other services or a referral to any medical specialists.

Ezekial's EI providers discussed with Latoya their knowledge and experiences related to hand flapping. Like toe walking, hand flapping is commonly observed in young children with autism. In the authors' experience, hand flapping often occurs when the children are excited. In many cases, the children do not readily exhibit joint or shared attention such as looks or expressions directed to others to convey feelings such as "Wow, this is great." Hand flapping often appears to be the manner in which the children express their pleasure, surprise, or other emotions that they feel but do not share with others. Often when the children become more interactive and more communicative, the hand flapping diminishes.

Feces smearing, another concern of Latoya's, has been reported in children with autism (Jang, Dixon, Tarbox, & Granpeesheh, 2011). The authors (Crawford & Weber) have worked with many children who smeared feces. In their experience, this behavior began when the children became more aware of their elimination. Many times, the children tried to get their feces out of their diaper when they were alone, and when they did so, they tried to wipe the mess off their hands. It seems they wanted the stool out of their diaper and did not have any way to communicate this desire to others. Depending on their sensory systems, some children found the sensation on their hands to be pleasurable and others did not, and this factor may have contributed to the frequency with which the feces smearing occurred. Another factor related to the frequency was the reaction the child received. Some children quickly learned that reaching into their diaper was an effective way to escape from or avoid naptime and/or to receive some attention. Parents who had a video monitor and saw their child reach into his or her diaper rushed into the child's room and changed the diaper before the child made a mess. Hence, one can see that Flexibility (the stool does not belong in the diaper); Making Sense of Self, Others, and the Environment (sensory factors); and Social Communication (challenges in telling others of the need for a diaper change) can all be factors in feces smearing. To stop the behavior, the parents found ways to keep the children from being able to reach into the diaper or take off their clothes, including using shirts that snapped at the crotch, applying tape around the top of the diaper (not on the skin) so it was loose enough for comfort but too tight for the child's hand to fit, or dressing the child in sleepers that the child could not remove. One resourceful parent hired a seamstress to move the zippers onto the back of the sleepers, and another dressed the child in a short-sleeved button-down shirt, which prevented the child from unzipping the zipper because he could not unbutton the shirt. In addition, some parents purchased commercially available clothing designed to be difficult or impossible for children to remove.

Latoya and the EI providers discussed ideas regarding Ezekial's stereotypies and brainstormed ways to help Latoya address her concerns regarding Ezekial's selective eating that would affect their trip. They decided to work on increasing Ezekial's variety of foods and his ability to sit and eat in a variety of settings, including at a local park, at a local fast-food restaurant, and at a casual family restaurant (see Chapter 7). To help him get accustomed to sitting in his car seat in new places, his team suggested Latoya bring his car seat into the house so Ezekial could sit in it for a variety of activities he enjoyed, such as watching movies and eating his favorite snacks.

Latoya was also concerned about Ezekial's ability to wait in line at the airport and at Disney World, and she worried that he would run away from her. Latoya and the EI providers brainstormed ways to engage Ezekial while he was waiting in line and also ways to reinforce his waiting. To prepare for this, they practiced at the post office, bank, and grocery store. On the first trip, the EI provider waited in line while Latoya and Ezekial walked nearby. When the EI provider was near the front of the line, Latoya and Ezekial joined them. On each subsequent practice session, Ezekial was required to wait a little longer. After several weeks, he was able to wait in line calmly for short amounts of time. The EI providers and Latoya also brainstormed about ways to address Ezekial's tendency to run away from her. They decided it would be beneficial for Latoya to help Ezekial practice when in the yard, when taking walks in the neighborhood, and when going out in the community. They discussed and practiced strategies including giving Ezekial choices such as "Hold my hand or sit in the stroller" and "Hold my hand or I will carry you." Whenever Ezekial let go of her hand, Latoya would put him in his stroller or carry him. Though Ezekial had tantrums the first few times he was put in the stroller, he quickly learned the rule. With the help of the EI providers coaching her in appropriate strategies, Latoya taught Ezekial to come when she called him, which gave Latoya more confidence about the trip.

When they returned from Disney World, Latoya reported that everyone had a great time, and she was amazed that she did not have to be "walking on eggshells" as she had been before Ezekial began in EI services. Though there were times when Ezekial's behavior was challenging, Latoya knew how to prevent many of his meltdowns, and she knew what she needed to do if they occurred. Ezekial's tantrums and aggressive behavior had decreased, and Latoya believed she was ready to tackle the next steps for Ezekial: sleeping in his own room all night and imitating actions, sounds, and words.

Ezekial's team had examined his strengths and needs related to the core deficits of autism. They helped Latoya manage Ezekial's behaviors and facilitate his skills.

PUTTING IT TOGETHER

Tables 9.1 and 9.2 provide examples of ways that EI providers and families can use this chapter's problem-solving approach. The examples show how to determine factors that may be affecting children in specific routines. Furthermore, the examples illustrate how EI providers and families can implement short-term and long-term strategies that assist children in responding in socially meaningful ways to their needs, the needs of others, and the demands of the environment.

Table 9.1. Activity: Outings in the community

Nora's behavior of concern	Core deficit to consider	What Nora may be responding to or thinking	Short-term solutions to consider	Long-term solutions to consider	Book chapter(s) to consult for more information
Nora pulls away when an adult holds her hand. She drops to her knees and cries when the adult persists.	Flexibility	I walk without holding others' hands.	Place Nora in her stroller or a shopping cart as soon as she gets out of the car. Give Nora the choice "Hold my hand or sit in the _____ (stroller or cart.)"	Target holding hands in a variety of settings. Begin with short amounts of time and gradually increase the expectations.	Chapter 5
	Making Sense of Self, Others, and the Environment	I don't know where we are going and what is expected of me.	Prepare Nora by showing her and telling her where she is going.	Take Nora on outings as often as possible so they become familiar.	Chapters 5 and 6
		I don't understand when you say, "Hold my hand."	Use consistent language and say, "Hold my hand" as you take her hand.	Take pictures and make a book about her trips to various places in the community.	
		I don't like how it feels when someone holds my hand.	Have Nora wear a backpack that an adult can hold onto.	Target following the direction "Hold my hand" throughout a variety of daily routines. Hold Nora's hands during activities she enjoys to help her tolerate the feeling and so she associates the feeling with preferred activities.	
	Social Communication	I don't have a way to tell you I don't want to hold your hand.	Let Nora know that her message was received but that she does not have a choice by saying, "I know you want to let go, but you need to hold my hand."	Target gestures and words that are appropriate ways to protest, such as shaking the head for "no" or holding out the hand to indicate "stop" as well as following directions.	Chapters 5 and 8
Nora makes loud, inappropriate noises.	Making Sense of Self, Others, and the Environment	I don't understand that I need to be quiet here.	Give Nora something to do that is incompatible with making noises, such as biting on a chewy toy, eating a snack, or drinking.	Target following the direction "Shhh, quiet" in a variety of routines. During play, practice banging loudly and quietly to help Nora understand the difference.	Chapters 5 and 6
	Social Communication	I want attention.	Give Nora attention when she is momentarily quiet.	Teach Nora how to gain attention appropriately such as by tapping others or calling others' names.	Chapters 5 and 8
Nora has tantrums or tries to leave when it is time to wait.	Making Sense of Self, Others, and the Environment	I want something now, and I don't think I am going to get it.	When waiting is required, before Nora gets dysregulated, distract her by singing a familiar song or giving her a toy, book, or snack.	Target waiting during a variety of daily routines by working on "First _____, then _____." Help Nora learn to wait, first for just seconds for something unimportant to her (e.g., "Wait while I put toothpaste on your brush") and later for increasingly important things, gradually extending the time.	Chapters 5 and 6
	Social Communication	I want something now, but I don't know how to tell you.	Model "I want _____" or "_____ please" to acknowledge Nora's message. Tell her it is coming.	Target requesting using gestures and/or words.	Chapters 5 and 8

Note: Additional strategies can be found in Chapters 4–6 and Appendix A of *Early Intervention Every Day! Embedding Activities in Daily Routines for Young Children and Their Families* (Crawford & Weber, 2014).

Table 9.2. Activity: Attending a birthday party

Erik's behavior of concern	Core deficit to consider	What Erik may be responding to or thinking	Short-term solutions to consider	Long-term solutions to consider	Book chapter(s) to consult for more information
Erik goes to the door and cries.	Flexibility	Usually when I go to this house, I get to play outside. I am not supposed to be inside now.	Take Erik outside for a few minutes and then entice him inside using a preferred item.	Gradually vary routines and target interacting and playing with peers.	Chapters 5 and 7
		My movie is in the car. I want to go watch it.	Allow Erik to watch the movie in the house.	Target "First ____, then ____" in a variety of routines.	
	Making Sense of Self, Others, and the Environment	I don't know what is happening. I want to leave.	Give visual cues, warnings, and explanations to help Erik know what will happen.	Provide a variety of experiences to broaden Erik's repertoire.	Chapters 5 and 6
		I don't like it when people sing.	During the singing, take him to another room and close the door.	Desensitize Erik by singing during daily routines. First sing softly and for short periods of time, gradually increasing the volume and the duration.	
		I see balloons. I get scared when they pop.	Ask if the balloons can be moved.	Desensitize Erik to balloons by pointing to them in stores, looking at them in books, hanging them across the room and then gradually hanging them closer to him and playing with them in a way he finds amusing.	
	Social Communication	I want to leave.	Leave.	Target requesting using gestures and words such as "Bye-bye" and "All done" as well as "First ____, then ____."	Chapters 5 and 8
		I don't have my cup, and I am thirsty. There, isn't any way for me to tell anyone.	Anticipate needs by bringing his cup and giving it to him.	Target requesting by using gestures and words such as handing others Erik's cup, pulling others to the refrigerator, handing others a picture of a cup, using the sign, or saying "drink."	
		Mom isn't in the room, and I don't know how to get her.	Anticipate needs by having Mom tell Erik she is leaving and will be right back.	Target calling Mom using a gesture, using a sign, or saying the word "Mom."	
Erik refuses to eat the food on his plate.	Flexibility	I don't like this food. The food is not on *my* plate, and the drink is not in *my* cup.	Bring food Erik likes as well as his preferred cup, plate, and utensils.	Target accepting new foods and different plates, spoons, and cups.	Chapters 5 and 7
	Social Communication	I want other foods I see.	Give choices of foods.	Target "First ____, then ____" in a variety of routines. Target requesting by using gestures, signs, and words.	Chapters 5 and 8
Erik does not participate in activities with peers at the party.	Flexibility	I play in the same way with the same things no matter where I am.	Allow Erik to play by himself.	Expand Erik's play repertoire.	Chapters 5 and 7

(continued)

Table 9.2. *(continued)*

Erik's behavior of concern	Core deficit to consider	What Erik may be responding to or thinking	Short-term solutions to consider	Long-term solutions to consider	Book chapter(s) to consult for more information
	Making Sense of Self, Others, and the Environment	I don't like the noise that the children are making.	Allow Erik to play by himself or allow him to play by himself after spending a brief period of time with others.	Desensitize Erik by exposing him to other children for gradually increasing amounts of time, beginning with quiet settings such as the library and open areas such as the park, and then progressing to noisier settings.	Chapters 5 and 6
		I don't know how to play with the other children or with those toys.	Allow Erik to play by himself or help him play with the toys. Have peers give Erik items of interest.	Provide experience with peers, beginning with brief periods of parallel play, and progress to more interactive play. Target imitation of actions. Target play skills with objects. Practice games and activities at home and then in new settings.	
	Social Communication	I don't know what to say or do to interact.	Allow Erik to entertain himself in his typical manner. For a short time, help Erik participate with peers and then allow him to return to his preferred activity. Model words and, if needed, provide physical assistance for Erik to use gestures such as HI and BYE. Help Erik cheer or clap at the end of activities so that he can be part of the shared excitement.	Target imitation, turn taking, and direction following, including looking at peers and giving to peers.	Chapters 5 and 8

Note: Additional strategies can be found in Chapters 4–6 and Appendix A of *Early Intervention Every Day! Embedding Activities in Daily Routines for Young Children and Their Families* (Crawford & Weber, 2014).

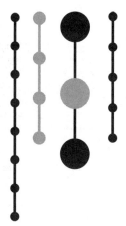

References

Abbott, M., Bernard, P., & Forge, J. (2013). Communicating a diagnosis of autism spectrum disorder—A qualitative study of parents' experiences. *Clinical Child Psychology and Psychiatry, 18*(3), 370–382. doi:10.1177/1359104512455813

Accardo, P.J., & Barrow, W. (2015). Toe walking in autism: Further observations. *Journal of Child Neurology, 30*(5), 606–609. doi:10.1177/0883073814521298

Accardo, P.J., Monasterio, E., & Oswald, D. (2014). Toe walking in autism. In V.B. Patel, V.R. Preedy, & C.R. Martin (Eds.), *Comprehensive guide to autism* (pp. 519–532). New York, NY: Springer.

Adams, C. (2005). Social communication intervention for school-age children: Rationale and description. *Seminars in Speech and Language, 26*(3), 181–188. doi:10.1055/s-2005-917123

Ahearn, W.H., Castine, T., Nault, K., & Green, G. (2001). An assessment of food acceptance in children with autism or pervasive developmental disorder-not otherwise specified. *Journal of Autism and Developmental Disorders, 31,* 505–511. doi:10.1023/A:1012221026124

American Psychiatric Association. (2013). *Diagnostic and statistical manual of mental disorders* (5th ed.). Arlington, VA: American Psychiatric Publishing.

American Speech-Language-Hearing Association. (2007a). *Childhood apraxia of speech.* Rockville, MD: Author.

American Speech-Language-Hearing Association. (2007b). *Scope of practice in speech-language-pathology.* Rockville, MD: Author.

American Speech-Language-Hearing Association. (2015a). *Components of social communication.* Retrieved from http://www.asha.org/uploadedFiles/ASHA/Practice_Portal/Clinical_Topics/Social_Communication_Disorders_in_School-Age_Children/Components-of-Social-Communication.pdf

American Speech-Language-Hearing Association. (2015b). *Social communication benchmarks.* Retrieved from http://www.asha.org/uploadedFiles/ASHA/Practice_Portal/Clinical_Topics/Social_Communication_Disorders_in_School-Age_Children/Social-Communication-Benchmarks.pdf

American Speech-Language-Hearing Association. (2015c). *Social communication disorders in school-age children.* Retrieved from http://www.asha.org/Practice-Portal/Clinical-Topics/Social-Communication-Disorders-in-School-Age-Children/

Anagnostou, E., Jones, N., Huerta, M., Halladay, A.K., Wang, P., Scahill, L., ... Dawson, G. (2015). Measuring social communication behaviors as a treatment endpoint in individuals with autism spectrum disorder. *Autism, 19*(5), 622–636. doi:10.1177/1362361314542955

Ashburner, J.K., Rodger, S.A., Ziviani, J.M., & Hinder, E.A. (2014). Comment on: "An intervention for sensory difficulties in children with autism: A randomized trial" by Schaaf et al. (2013). *Journal of Autism and Developmental Disorders, 44*(6), 1486–1488. doi:10.1007/s10803-014-2083-0

Autism Speaks. (2015a). *The Early Start Denver Model (ESDM).* Retrieved from http://www.autismspeaks.org/what-autism/treatment/early-start-denver-model-esdm

Autism Speaks. (2015b). *Learn the signs of autism.* Retrieved from http://www.autismspeaks.org/what-autism/learn-signs

Ayres, A.J. (1972). *Sensory integration and learning disorders.* Los Angeles, CA: Western Psychological Services.

Ayres, A.J. (1979). *Sensory integration and the child.* Los Angeles, CA: Western Psychological Services.

Ayres, A.J. (1985, May). *Developmental dyspraxia and adult-onset apraxia.* Paper presented at the meeting of Sensory Integration International, Torrance, CA.

Bahrick, L.E., & Lickliter, R. (2014). Learning to attend selectively: The dual role of intersensory redundancy. *Current Directions in Psychological Science, 23*(6), 414–420. doi:10.1177/0963721414549187

Bailey, K. (2008). Supporting families. In K. Chawarska, A. Klin, & F.R. Volkmar (Eds.), *Autism spectrum disorders in infants and toddlers: Diagnosis, assessment, and treatment* (pp. 300–326). New York, NY: Guilford Press.

Baranek, G.T., Little, L.M., Parham, L.D., Ausderau, K.K., & Sabatos-DeVito, M.G. (2014). Sensory features in autism spectrum disorders. In F.R. Volkmar, S.J. Rogers, R. Paul, & K.A. Pelphrey (Eds.), *Handbook of autism and pervasive developmental disorders:*

Diagnosis, development, and brain mechanisms (4th ed., Vol. 1, pp. 378–407). Hoboken, NJ: Wiley.

Barbera, M.L. (2007). *The verbal behavior approach: How to teach children with autism and related disorders*. Philadelphia, PA: Jessica Kingsley.

Barrett, K.C. (2013). Introduction to section one: Overview and analysis. In K.C. Barrett, N.A. Fox, G.A. Morgan, D.J. Fidler, & L.A. Daunhauer (Eds.), *Handbook of self-regulatory processes in development: New directions and international perspectives* (pp. 3-4). New York, NY: Psychology Press.

Beier, J.S., & Spelke, E.S. (2012). Infants' developing understanding of social gaze. *Child Development, 83*(2), 486–496. doi:10.1111/j.1467-8624.2011.01702.x

Ben-Sasson, A., Soto, T.W., Martínez-Pedraza, F., & Carter, A.S. (2013). Early sensory over-responsivity in toddlers with autism spectrum disorders as a predictor of family impairment and parenting stress. *Journal of Child Psychology and Psychiatry, 54*(8), 846–853. doi:10.1111/jcpp.12035

Berger, N.I., & Ingersoll, B. (2014). A further investigation of goal-directed intention understanding in young children with autism spectrum disorders. *Journal of Autism and Developmental Disorders, 44*(12), 3204–3214. doi:10.1007/s10803-014-2181-z

Bondy, A.S., & Frost, L.A. (1994). The Picture Exchange Communication System. *Focus on Autism and Other Developmental Disabilities, 9*(3), 1–19. doi:10.1177/108835769400900301

Bottema-Beutel, K., Yoder, P., Woynaroski, T., & Sandbank, M.P. (2014). Targeted interventions for social communication symptoms in preschoolers with autism spectrum disorders. In F.R. Volkmar, S.J. Rogers, R. Paul, & K.A. Pelphrey (Eds.), *Handbook of autism and pervasive developmental disorders: Assessment, interventions, and policy* (4th ed., Vol. 2, pp. 788–812). Hoboken, NJ: Wiley.

Boulter, C., Freeston, M., South, M., & Rodgers, J. (2014). Intolerance of uncertainty as a framework for understanding anxiety in children and adolescents with autism spectrum disorders. *Journal of Autism and Developmental Disorders, 44*(6), 1391–1402. doi:10.1007/s10803-013-2001-x

Boyd, B.A., Odom, S.L., Humphreys, B.P., & Sam, A.M. (2010). Infants and toddlers with autism spectrum disorder: Early identification and early intervention. *Journal of Early Intervention, 32*(2), 75–98. doi:10.1177/1053815110362690

Bradford, K. (2010). Supporting families dealing with autism and Asperger's disorders. *Journal of Family Psychotherapy, 21,* 149–156. doi:10.1080/08975353.2010.483660

Brian, J.A., Bryson, S.E., & Zwaigenbaum, L. (2015). Autism spectrum disorder in infancy: Developmental considerations in treatment targets. *Current Opinion in Neurology, 28*(2), 117–123. doi:10.1097/WCO.0000000000000182

Briggs-Gowan, M.J., Carter, A.S., Irwin, J.R., Wachtel, K., Cicchetti, D.V. (2004). The Brief Infant–Toddler Social and Emotional Assessment: Screening for social-emotional problems and delays in competence. *Journal of Pediatric Psychology, 29*(2), 143–155. doi:10.1093/jpepsy/jsh017

Bruinsma, Y., Koegel, R.L., & Koegel, L.K. (2004). Joint attention and children with autism: A review of the literature. *Mental Retardation and Developmental Disabilities Research Reviews, 10*(3), 169–175. doi:10.1002/mrdd.20036

Bruner, J. (1981). The social context of language acquisition. *Language and Communication, 1*(2), 155–178. doi:10.1016/0271-5309(81)90010-0

Calkins, S.D. (2007). The emergence of self-regulation: Biological and behavioral control mechanisms supporting toddler competencies. In C.A. Brownell & C.B. Kopp (Eds.), *Socioemotional development in the toddler years: Transitions and transformations* (pp. 261–284). New York, NY: Guilford Press.

Cameron, M.J., Ainsleigh, S.A., & Bird, F.L. (1992). The acquisition of stimulus control of compliance and participation during an ADL routine. *Behavioral Residential Treatment, 7*(5), 327–340. doi:10.1002/bin.2360070502

Carter, A.S., Messinger, D.S., Stone, W.L., Celimli, S., Nahmias, A.S., & Yoder, P. (2011). A randomized controlled trial of Hanen's 'More than Words' in toddlers with early autism symptoms. *Journal of Child Psychology and Psychiatry, 52*(7), 741–752. doi:10.1111/j.1469-7610.2011.02395.x

Case-Smith, J., Weaver, L.L., & Fristad, M.A. (2014). A systematic review of sensory processing interventions for children with autism spectrum disorders. *Autism, 19*(2), 133–148. doi:10.1177/1362361313517762

Casenhiser, D.M., Shanker, S.G., & Stieben, J. (2013). Learning through interaction in children with autism: Preliminary data from a social-communication-based intervention. *Autism, 17*(2), 220–241. doi:10.1177/1362361311422052

Casey, L.B., Zanksas, S., Meindl, J.N., Parra, G.R., Cogdal, P., & Powell, K. (2012). Parental symptoms of post-traumatic stress following a child's diagnosis of autism spectrum disorder: A pilot study. *Research in Autism Spectrum Disorders, 6*(3), 1186–1193. doi:10.1016/j.rasd.2012.03.008

Centers for Disease Control and Prevention. (n.d.). *Tips for talking with parents.* Retrieved from http://www.cdc.gov/ncbddd/actearly/pdf/parents_pdfs/TipsTalkingParents.pdf

Centers for Disease Control and Prevention. (2014). *Autism spectrum disorder (ASD): Signs and symptoms.* Retrieved from http://www.cdc.gov/ncbddd/autism/signs.html

Colgan, S.E., Lanter, E., McComish, C., Watson, L.R., Crais, E.R., & Baranek, G.T. (2006). Analysis of social interaction gestures in infants with autism. *Child Neuropsychology, 12*(4–5), 307–319. doi:10.1080/09297040600701360

Cooper, J.O., Heron, T.E., & Heward, W.L. (2007). *Applied behavior analysis.* Upper Saddle River, NJ: Pearson.

Cossu, G., Boria, S., Copioli, C., Bracceschi, R., Giuberti, V., Santelli, E.,. Gallese, V. (2012). Motor representation of actions in children with autism. *PLoS ONE, 7*(9), e44779. doi:10.1371/journal.pone.0044779

Crais, E., Douglas, D.D., & Campbell, C.C. (2004). The intersection of the development of gestures and intentionality. *Journal of Speech, Language, and*

Hearing Research, 47(3), 678–694. doi:10.1044/1092-4388(2004/052

Crais, E.R., Watson, L.R., & Baranek, G.T. (2009). Use of gesture development in profiling children's prelinguistic communication skills. *American Journal of Speech-Language Pathology, 18*(1), 95–108. doi:10.1044/1058-0360(2008/07-0041)

Crawford, M.J., & Weber, B. (2014). *Early intervention every day! Embedding activities in daily routines for young children and their families.* Baltimore, MD: Paul H. Brookes Publishing Co.

Daniels, A.M., & Mandell, D.S. (2014). Explaining differences in age at autism spectrum disorder diagnosis: A critical review. *Autism, 18*(5), 583–597. doi:10.1177/1362361313480277

D'Cruz, A., Ragozzino, M.E., Mosconi, M.W., Shrestha, S., Cook, E.H., & Sweeney, J.A. (2013). Reduced behavioral flexibility in autism spectrum disorders. *Neuropsychology, 27*(2), 152–160. doi:10.1037/a0031721

Deák, G.O. (2004). The development of cognitive flexibility and language abilities. *Advances in Child Development and Behavior, 31,* 271–327. doi:10.1016/S0065-2407(03)31007-9

DeGangi, G. (2000). *Pediatric disorders of regulation in affect and behavior: A therapist's guide to assessment and treatment.* San Diego, CA: Academic Press.

Delmolino, L., & Harris, S.L. (2004). *Incentives for change: Motivating people with autism spectrum behaviors to learn and gain independence.* Bethesda, MD: Woodbine House.

DeWeerdt, S. (2014). *Lack of training begets autism diagnosis bottleneck.* Retrieved from http://sfari.org/news-and-opinion/news/2014/lack-of-training-begets-autism-diagnosis-bottleneck

Dewey, D. (1995). What is developmental dyspraxia? *Brain and Cognition, 29*(3), 254–274. doi:10.1006/brcg.1995.1281

Di Pietro, N.C., Whiteley, L., Mizgalewicz, A., & Illes, J. (2013). Treatments for neurodevelopmental disorders: Evidence, advocacy, and the Internet. *Journal of Autism and Developmental Disorders, 43*(1), 122–133. doi:10.1007/s10803-012-1551-7

Dicker, S. (2013). Entering the spectrum: The challenge of early intervention law for children with autism spectrum disorders. *Infants & Young Children, 26*(3), 192–203. doi:10.1097/IYC.0b013e3182953081

Duff, C.K., & Flattery, J.J., Jr. (2014). Developing mirror self awareness in students with autism spectrum disorder. *Journal of Autism and Developmental Disorders, 44*(5), 1027–1038. doi:10.1007/s10803-013-1954-0

Dunphy-Lelii, S., LaBounty, J., Lane, J.D., & Wellman, H.M. (2014). The social context of infant intention understanding. *Journal of Cognition and Development, 15*(1), 60–77. doi:10.1080/15248372.2012.710863

Dunst, C.J., Trivette, C.M., & Hamby, D.W. (2007). Meta-analysis of family-centered helpgiving practices research. *Mental Retardation and Developmental Disabilities Research Reviews, 13*(4), 370–378. doi:10.1002/mrdd.20176

Durand, V.M. (2011). *Optimistic parenting: Hope and help for you and your challenging child.* Baltimore, MD: Paul H. Brookes Publishing Co.

Durand, V.M. (2014, October). *Optimistic parenting: Hope and help for individuals with challenging behavior.* Presentation at 32nd Annual Autism Conference, Atlantic City, NJ.

El-Sheikh, M., & Sadeh, A. (2015). I. Sleep and development: Introduction to the monograph. *Monographs of the Society for Research in Child Development, 80*(1), 1–14. doi:10.1111/mono.12141

Ennis-Cole, D., Durodoye, B.A., & Harris, H.L. (2013). The impact of culture on autism diagnosis and treatment: Considerations for counselors and other professionals. *The Family Journal, 21*(3), 279–287. doi:10.1177/1066480713476834

Ewles, G., Clifford, T., & Minnes, P. (2014). Predictors of advocacy in parents of children with autism spectrum disorders. *Journal on Developmental Disabilities, 20*(1), 73–82.

Fabbri-Destro, M., Gizzonio, V., & Avanzini, P. (2013). Autism, motor dysfunctions and mirror mechanism. *Clinical Neuropsychiatry, 10*(5), 177–187.

Faedda, G.L., Baldessarini, R.J., Glovinsky, I.P., & Austin, N.B. (2004). Pediatric bipolar disorder: Phenomenology and course of illness. *Bipolar Disorders, 6*(4), 305–313. doi:10.1111/j.1399-5618.2004.00128.x

Falkmer, T., Anderson, K., Falkmer, M., & Horlin, C. (2013). Diagnostic procedures in autism spectrum disorders: A systematic literature review. *European Child and Adolescent Psychiatry, 22*(6), 329–340. doi:10.1007/s00787-013-0375-0

Fodstad, J.C., Rojahn, J., & Matson, J.L. (2012). The emergence of challenging behaviors in at-risk toddlers with and without autism spectrum disorder: A cross-sectional study. *Journal of Developmental and Physical Disabilities, 24*(3), 217–234. doi:10.1007/s10882-011-9266-9

Fogel, A. (1993). *Developing through relationships.* Chicago, IL: University of Chicago.

Forssman, L. (2012). *Attention and the early development of cognitive control: Infants' and toddlers' performance on the A-not-B task* (Doctoral dissertation, University of Tampere, Finland). Retrieved from http://www.uta.fi/med/icl/people/linda/Doctoral%20thesis.pdf

Foss-Feig, J.H., Heacock, J.L., & Cascio, C.J. (2012). Tactile responsiveness patterns and their association with core features in autism spectrum disorders. *Research in Autism Spectrum Disorders, 6*(1), 337–344. doi:10.1016/j.rasd.2011.06.007

Gensler, D. (2009). Initiative and advocacy when a parent has a child with a disability. *Journal of Infant, Child, and Adolescent Psychotherapy, 8*(1), 57–69. doi:10.1080/15289160802683484

Gianino, A., & Tronick, E.Z. (1988). The mutual regulation model: The infants' self and interactive regulation and coping and defensive capacities. In T.M. Field, P.M. McCabe, & N. Schneiderman (Eds.), *Stress and coping across development* (pp. 47–68). Hillsdale, NJ: Erlbaum.

Gibson, J.J. (1979). *The ecological approach to visual perception.* Boston, MA: Houghton Mifflin.

Gillis, R., & Nilsen, E.S. (2014). Cognitive flexibility supports preschoolers' detection of communicative ambiguity. *First Language, 34*(1), 58–71. doi:10.1177/0142723714521839

Goldin-Meadow, S., & Alibali, M.W. (2013). Gesture's role in speaking, learning, and creating language. *Annual Review of Psychology, 64,* 257. doi:10.1146/annurev-psych-113011-143802

Goodwyn, S.W., Acredolo, L.P., & Brown, C.A. (2000). Impact of symbolic gesturing on early language development. *Journal of Nonverbal Behavior, 24*(2), 81–103. doi:10.1023/A:1006653828895

Grandin, T. (2002, August). Teaching people with autism/Asperger's to be more flexible. *Autism Today.* Retrieved from http://www.autismtoday.com/library-back/Teaching_Flexibility.htm

Grandin, T. (2011, November/December). Why do kids with autism stim? *Autism Asperger's Digest.* Retrieved from http://autismdigest.com/why-do-kids-with-autism-stim/

Green, S.A., Rudie, J.D., Colich, N.L., Wood, J.J., Shirinyan, D., Hernandez, L., ... Bookheimer, S.Y. (2013). Overreactive brain responses to sensory stimuli in youth with autism spectrum disorders. *Journal of the American Academy of Child and Adolescent Psychiatry, 52*(11), 1158–1172. doi:10.1016/j.jaac.2013.08.004

Griffin, P., Peters, M.L., & Smith, R.M. (2007). Ableism curriculum design. In M. Adams, L.A. Belle, & P. Griffin (Eds.), *Teaching for diversity and social justice* (2nd ed., pp. 335–358). New York, NY: Taylor & Francis.

Gulick, R., & Kitchen, T. (2007). *Effective instruction for children with autism: An applied behavior analytic approach.* Erie, PA: The Dr. Gertrude A. Barber National Institute.

Guthrie, W., Swineford, L.B., Nottke, C., & Wetherby, A.M. (2013). Early diagnosis of autism spectrum disorder: Stability and change in clinical diagnosis and symptom presentation. *Journal of Child Psychology and Psychiatry, 54*(5), 582–590. doi:10.1111/jcpp.12008

Gutstein, S.E., & Sheely, R.K. (2002). *Relationship development intervention with young children.* London, United Kingdom: Jessica Kingsley.

Hazen, E.P., Stornelli, J.L., O'Rourke, J.A., Koesterer, K., & McDougle, C.J. (2014). Sensory symptoms in autism spectrum disorders. *Harvard Review of Psychiatry, 22*(2), 112–124. doi:10.1097/01.HRP.0000445143.08773.58

Hellendoorn, A., Langstraat, I., Wijnroks, L., Buitelaar, J.K., van Daalen, E., & Leseman, P.P. (2014). The relationship between atypical visual processing and social skills in young children with autism. *Research in Developmental Disabilities, 35*(2), 423–428. doi:10.1016/j.ridd.2013.11.012

Henrichs, J., & Van den Bergh, B.R. (2015). Perinatal developmental origins of self-regulation. In G.H.E. Gendolla, M. Tops, & S.L. Koole (Eds.), *Handbook of biobehavioral approaches to self-regulation* (pp. 349–370). New York, NY: Springer.

Higgins, D.J., Bailey, S.R., & Pearce, J.C. (2005). Factors associated with functioning style and coping strategies of families with a child with an autism spectrum disorder. *Autism: The International Journal of Research and Practice, 9*(2), 125–137. doi:10.1177/1362361305051403

Hood, B.M. (1995). Visual selective attention in the human infant: A neuroscientific approach. In C. Rovee-Collier, L. Lipsitt, & H. Hayne (Eds.), *Advances in infancy research* (pp. 163–216). Norwood, NJ: Ablex.

Hoyson, M., Jamieson, B., & Strain, P.S. (1984). Individualized group instruction of normally developing and autistic-like children: The LEAP curriculum model. *Journal of the Division for Early Childhood, 8,* 157–172.

Hwa-Froelich, D.A. (Ed.). (2015). *Social communication development and disorders.* New York, NY: Taylor and Francis.

Individuals with Disabilities Education Improvement Act (IDEA) of 2004, PL 108-446, 20 U.S.C. §§ 1400 *et seq.*

Ishak, S., Franchak, J.M., & Adolph, K.E. (2014). Perception–action development from infants to adults: Perceiving affordances for reaching through openings. *Journal of Experimental Child Psychology, 117,* 92–105. doi:10.1016/j.jecp.2013.09.003

Jang, J., Dixon, D.R., Tarbox, J., & Granpeesheh, D. (2011). Symptom severity and challenging behavior in children with ASD. *Research in Autism Spectrum Disorders, 5*(3), 1028–1032. doi:10.1016/j.rasd.2010.11.008

Johnson, C.P., & Myers, S.M. (2007). Identification and evaluation of children with autism spectrum disorders. *Pediatrics, 120*(5), 1183–1215. doi:10.1542/peds.2007-2361

Jones, W., & Klin, A. (2013). Attention to eyes is present but in decline in 2–6-month-old infants later diagnosed with autism. *Nature, 504*(7480), 427–431. doi:10.1038/nature12715

Kanner, L. (1943). Autistic disturbances of affective contact. *Nervous Child, 2,* 217–250. Retrieved from http://simonsfoundation.s3.amazonaws.com/share/071207-leo-kanner-autistic-affective-contact.pdf

Kasari, C., Gulsrud, A.C., Wong, C., Kwon, S., & Locke, J. (2010). Randomized controlled caregiver mediated joint engagement intervention for toddlers with autism. *Journal of Autism and Developmental Disorders, 40,* 1045–1056. doi:10.1007/s10803-010-0955-5

Kenworthy, L., Case, L., Harms, M.B., Martin, A., & Wallace, G.L. (2010). Adaptive behavior ratings correlate with symptomatology and IQ among individuals with high-functioning autism spectrum disorders. *Journal of Autism and Developmental Disorders, 40*(4), 416–423. doi:10.1007/s10803-009-0911-4.

Kern, J.K., Geier, D.A., & Geier, M.R. (2014). Evaluation of regression in autism spectrum disorder based on parental reports. *North American Journal of Medical Sciences, 6*(1), 41–47. doi:10.4103/1947-2714.125867

Kerwin, M.E., Eicher, P.S., & Gelsinger, J. (2005). Parental report of eating problems and gastrointestinal symptoms in children with pervasive developmental disorders. *Child Health Care, 34*(3), 221–234. doi:10.1207/s15326888chc3403_4

Kim, S.H., Paul, R., Tager-Flusberg, H., & Lord, C. (2014). Language and communication in autism. In F.R. Volkmar, R. Paul, S.J. Rogers, & K.A. Pelphrey (Eds.), *Handbook of autism and pervasive developmental disorders: Diagnosis, development, and brain mechanisms* (4th ed., Vol. 1, pp. 230–262). Hoboken, NJ: Wiley.

Klin, A., Shultz, S., & Jones, W. (2015). Social visual engagement in infants and toddlers with autism: Early developmental transitions and a model of pathogenesis. *Neuroscience and Biobehavioral Reviews, 50,* 189–203. doi:10.1016/j.neubiorev.2014.10.006

Klintwall, L., Macari, S., Eikeseth, S., & Chawarska, K. (2014). Interest level in 2-year-olds with autism spectrum disorder predicts rate of verbal, nonverbal, and adaptive skill acquisition. *Autism, 19*(8), 925–933. doi:10.1177/1362361314555376

Koegel, L.K., Park, M.N., & Koegel, R.L. (2014). Using self-management to improve the reciprocal social conversation of children with autism spectrum disorder. *Journal of Autism and Developmental Disorders, 44*(5), 1055–1063. doi:10.1007/s10803-013-1956-y

Koegel, R.L., & Koegel, L.K. (2012). *The PRT pocket guide: Pivotal Response Treatment for autism.* Baltimore, MD: Paul H. Brookes Publishing Co.

Konst, M.J., Matson, J.L., & Turygin, N. (2013). Exploration of the correlation between autism spectrum disorder symptomology and tantrum behaviors. *Research in Autism Spectrum Disorders, 7*(9), 1068–1074. doi:10.1016/j.rasd.2013.05.006

Kopp, C.B. (1982). Antecedents of self-regulation: A developmental perspective. *Developmental Psychology, 18*(2), 199–214. doi:10.1037/0012-1649.18.2.199

Landa, R.J., Holman, K.C., O'Neil, A.H., & Stuart, E.A. (2011). Intervention targeting development of socially synchronous engagement in toddlers with autism spectrum disorder: A randomized controlled trial. *Journal of Child Psychology and Psychiatry, 52*(1), 13–21. doi:10.1111/j.1469-7610.2010.02288.x

Landry, R., & Bryson, S.E. (2004). Impaired disengagement of attention in young children with autism. *Journal of Child Psychology and Psychiatry, 45*(6), 1115–1122. doi:10.1111/j.1469-7610.2004.00304.x

Lane, S.J., Ivey, C.K., & May-Benson, T.A. (2014). Test of Ideational Praxis (TIP): Preliminary findings and interrater and test-retest reliability with preschoolers. *American Journal of Occupational Therapy, 68*(5), 555–561. doi:10.5014/ajot.2014.012542

Lang, R., O'Reilly, M., Healy, O., Rispoli, M., Lydon, H., Streusand, W., … Giesbersi, S. (2012). Sensory integration therapy for autism spectrum disorders: A systematic review. *Research in Autism Spectrum Disorders, 6*(3), 1004–1018. doi:10.1016/j.rasd.2012.01.006

Leach, D. (2012). *Bringing ABA to home, school, and play for young children with autism spectrum disorders and other disabilities.* Baltimore, MD: Paul H. Brookes Publishing Co.

Leung, R.C., & Zakzanis, K.K. (2014). Brief report: Cognitive flexibility in autism spectrum disorders: A quantitative review. *Journal of Autism and Developmental Disorders, 44*(10), 2628–2645. doi:10.1007/s10803-014-2136-4

Linkenauger, S.A., Lerner, M.D., Ramenzoni, V.C., & Proffitt, D.R. (2012). A perceptual–motor deficit predicts social and communicative impairments in individuals with autism spectrum disorders. *Autism Research, 5*(5), 352–362. doi:10.1002/aur.1248

Lipsky, D. (2011). *From anxiety to meltdown: How individuals on the autism spectrum deal with anxiety, experience meltdowns, manifest tantrums, and how you can intervene effectively.* London, United Kingdom: Jessica Kingsley.

Lord, C., Rutter, M., DiLavore, P., Risi, S., Gotham, K., & Bishop, S.L. (2012). *Autism Diagnostic Observation Schedule (ADOS-2): Manual* (2nd ed.). Los Angeles, CA: Western Psychological Services.

Lovaas, O.I. (1987). Behavioral treatment and normal educational and intellectual functioning in young autistic children. *Journal of Consulting and Clinical Psychology, 55*(1), 3–9. Retrieved from http://dddc.rutgers.edu/pdf/lovaas.pdf

Lynch, E.W., & Hanson, M.J. (2011). *Developing cross-cultural competence: A guide for working with children and their families* (4th ed.). Baltimore, MD: Paul H. Brookes Publishing Co.

Lyons, V., & Fitzgerald, M. (2013). Atypical sense of self in autism spectrum disorders: A neuro-cognitive perspective. In M. Fitzgerald (Ed.), *Recent advances in autism spectrum disorders* (Vol. 1). Rijeka, Croatia: InTech. Retrieved from http://www.intechopen.com/books/recent-advances-in-autism-spectrum-disorders-volume-i/atypical-sense-of-self-in-autism-spectrum-disorders-a-neuro-cognitive-perspective

MacDuff, G.S., Krantz, P.J., & McClannahan, L.E. (2001). Prompts and prompt-fading strategies for people with autism. In G. Green & C. Maurice (Eds.), *Making a difference: Behavioral intervention for autism* (pp. 37–50). Austin, TX: PRO-ED.

Mace, F.C., Hock, M.L., Lalli, J.S., West, B.J., Belfiore, P., Pinter, E., & Brown, D.K. (1988). Behavioral momentum in the treatment of noncompliance. *Journal of Applied Behavior Analysis, 21*(2), 123–141. doi:10.1901/jaba.1988.21-123

Mahoney, G., & MacDonald, J. (2005). *Responsive teaching: Parent-mediated developmental intervention.* Cleveland, OH: Case Western Reserve University.

Marco, E.J., Hinkley, L.B., Hill, S.S., & Nagarajan, S.S. (2011). Sensory processing in autism: A review of neurophysiologic findings. *Pediatric Research, 69*(5), 48R–54R. doi:10.1203/PDR.0b013e3182130c54

Marcus, L.M., Kunce, L.J., & Schopler, E. (2005). Working with families. In F.R. Volkmar, R. Paul, A. Klin, & D.J. Cohen (Eds.), *Handbook of autism and pervasive developmental disorders: Assessment, interventions, and policy* (3rd ed., Vol. 2, pp. 1055–1086). Hoboken, NJ: Wiley.

Marcus, L., & Schopler, E. (2007). Educational approaches for autism—TEACCH. In E. Hollander & E. Anagnostou (Eds.), *Autism spectrum clinical manual for the treatment of autism* (pp. 211–233). Washington, DC: American Psychiatric Publishing.

Matson, J.L., Adams, H.L., Williams, L.W., & Rieske, R.D. (2013). Why are there so many unsubstantiated treatments in autism? *Research in Autism Spectrum Disorders, 7*(3), 466–474. doi:10.1016/j.rasd.2012.11.006

Matson, J.L., Worley, J.A., Kozlowski, A.M., Chung, K., Jung, W., & Yang, J. (2012). Cross cultural differences of parent reported social skills in children with autistic disorder: An examination between South Korea and the United States of America. *Research in Autism Spectrum Disorders, 6*(3), 971–977. doi:10.1016/j.rasd.2011.07.019

Mayes, S.D., Calhoun, S., Bixler, E.O., & Vgontzas, A.N. (2009). Sleep problems in children with autism, ADHD, anxiety, depression, acquired brain injury, and typical development. *Sleep Medicine Clinics, 4*(1), 19–25. doi:10.1016/j.jsmc.2008.12.004

Mazefsky, C.A., Herrington, J., Siegel, M., Scarpa, A., Maddox, B.B., Scahill, L., & White, S.W. (2013). The role of emotion regulation in autism spectrum disorder. *Journal of the American Academy of Child and Adolescent Psychiatry, 52*(7), 679–688. doi:10.1016/j.jaac.2013.05.006

Mazurek, M.O., & Petroski, G.F. (2015). Sleep problems in children with autism spectrum disorder: Examining the contributions of sensory over-responsivity and anxiety. *Sleep Medicine, 16*(2), 270. doi:10.1016/j.sleep.2014.11.006

Mesibov, G.B., Shea, V., & Schopler, E. (2005). *The TEACCH approach to autism spectrum disorders.* New York, NY: Kluwer Academic/Plenum.

Mian, N.D., Godoy, L., Briggs-Gowan, M.J., & Carter, A.S. (2012). Patterns of anxiety symptoms in toddlers and preschool-age children: Evidence of early differentiation. *Journal of Anxiety Disorders, 26*(1), 102–110. doi:10.1016/j.janxdis.2011.09.006

Miniscalco, C., Rudling, M., Råstam, M., Gillberg, C., & Johnels, J.Å. (2014). Imitation (rather than core language) predicts pragmatic development in young children with ASD: A preliminary longitudinal study using CDI parental reports. *International Journal of Language and Communication Disorders, 49*(3), 369–375. doi:10.1111/1460-6984.12085

Mitchell, S., Brian, J., Zwaigenbaum, L., Roberts, W., Szatmari, P., Smith, I., & Bryson, S. (2006). Early language and communication development of infants later diagnosed with autism spectrum disorder. *Journal of Developmental and Behavioral Pediatrics, 27*(2), S69–S78. doi:10.1097/00004703-200604002-00004

Mody, M. (2014). Nonverbal individuals with autism spectrum disorder: Why don't they speak? *North American Journal of Medicine and Science, 7*(3), 130–134. doi:10.7156/najms. 2014.0703130

Mundy, P., & Jarrold, W. (2010). Infant joint attention, neural networks and social cognition. *Neural Networks, 23*(8), 985–997. doi:10.1016/j.neunet.2010.08.009

Mundy, P., & Newell, L. (2007). Attention, joint attention, and social cognition. *Current Directions in Psychological Science, 16*(5), 269–274. doi:10.1111/j.1467-8721.2007.00518.x

Muratori, F., Apicella, F., Muratori, P., & Maestro, S. (2011). Intersubjective disruptions and caregiver-infant interaction in early autistic disorder. *Research in Autism Spectrum Disorders, 5*(1), 408–417. doi:10.1016/j.rasd.2010.06.003

Myers, B.J., Mackintosh, V.H., & Goin-Kochel, R.P. (2009). "My greatest joy and my greatest heart ache": Parents' own words on how having a child in the autism spectrum has affected their lives and their families' lives. *Research in Autism Spectrum Disorders, 3*(3), 670–684. doi:10.1016/j.rasd.2009.01.004

Myers, S.M., & Johnson, C.J. (2007). Management of children with autism spectrum disorders. *Pediatrics, 120*, 1162–1182.

Nadel, J. (2014). *How imitation boosts development in infancy and autism spectrum disorder.* Oxford, United Kingdom: Oxford University Press.

National Research Council. (2001). *Educating children with autism.* Washington, DC: National Academy Press.

Nicholasen, M., & O'Neal, B. (2008). *I brake for meltdowns: How to handle the most exasperating behavior of your 2-to 5-year-old.* Boston, MA: Da Capo.

O'Connor, K. (2012). Auditory processing in autism spectrum disorder: A review. *Neuroscience and Biobehavioral Reviews, 36*(2), 836–854. doi:10.1016/j.neubiorev.2011.11.008

Odom, S.L., Boyd, B., Hall, L.J., & Hume, K. (2010). Evaluation of comprehensive treatment models for individuals with autism spectrum disorders. *Journal of Autism and Developmental Disabilities, 40*, 425–437. doi:10.1007/s10803-009-0825-1

Odom, S.L., Collet-Klingenberg, L., Rogers, S., & Hatton, D.D. (2010). Evidence-based practices in interventions for children and youth with autism spectrum disorders. *Preventing School Failure, 54*(4), 275–282. doi:10.1080/10459881003785506

Olswang, L.B., Coggins, T.E., & Timler, G.R. (2001). Outcome measures for school-age children with social communication problems. *Topics in Language Disorders, 22*(1), 50–73. doi:10.1097/00011363-200111000-00006

Ozonoff, S., Young, G.S., Carter, A., Messinger, D., Yirmiya, N., Zwaigenbaum, L., … Stone, W.L (2011). Recurrence risk for autism spectrum disorders: A Baby Siblings Research Consortium study. *Pediatrics, 128*(3), e488–e495. doi:10.1542/peds.2010-2825

Pang, Y. (2010). Facilitating family involvement in early intervention to preschool transition. *School Community Journal, 20*(2), 183–198. Retrieved from http://files.eric.ed.gov/fulltext/EJ908215.pdf

Parham, L.D., Cohn, E.S., Spitzer, S., Koomar, J.A., Miller, L.J., Burke, J.P., … Summers, C.A. (2007). Fidelity in sensory integration intervention research. *American Journal of Occupational Therapy, 61*(2), 216–227. doi:10.5014/ajot.61.2.216

Parham, L.D., & Mailloux, Z. (2015). Sensory integration. In J. Case-Smith & J.C. O'Brien (Eds.), *Occupational therapy for children and adolescents* (7th ed., pp. 258–303). St. Louis, MO: Elsevier.

Partington, J.W. (2008). *Capturing the motivation of children with autism or other developmental delays.* Walnut Creek, CA: Behavior Analysts.

Patten, E., Ausderau, K.K., Watson, L.R., & Baranek, G.T. (2013). Sensory response patterns in nonverbal children with ASD. *Autism Research and Treatment, 2013*, 1–9. doi:10.1155/2013/436286

Paul, R., Fuerst, Y., Ramsay, G., Chawarska, K., & Klin, A. (2011). Out of the mouths of babes: Vocal production in infant siblings of children with ASD. *Journal of Child Psychology and Psychiatry, 52*(5), 588–598. doi:10.1111/j.1469-7610.2010.02332.x

Pickles, A., Anderson, D.K., & Lord, C. (2014). Heterogeneity and plasticity in the development of language: A 17-year follow-up of children referred early for possible autism. *Journal of Child Psychology and Psychiatry, 55*(12), 1354–1362. doi:10.1111/jcpp.12269

Premack, D. (1959). Toward empirical behavioral laws: I. Positive reinforcement. *Psychological Review, 66*(4), 219–233. doi:10.1037/h0040891

Premack, D., & Woodruff, G. (1978). Does the chimpanzee have a theory of mind? *Behavioral and Brain Sciences, 1*(04), 515–526. doi:10.1017/S0140525X00076512

Prizant, B.M. (1983). Language acquisition and communicative behavior in autism: Toward an understanding of the whole of it. *Journal of Speech and Hearing Disorders, 48*(3), 296–307. doi:10.1044/jshd.4803.296

Prizant, B.M., Wetherby, A.M., Rubin, E., Laurent, A.C., & Rydell, P.J. (2006). *The SCERTS© Model: A comprehensive educational approach for children with autism spectrum disorders.* Baltimore, MD: Paul H. Brookes Publishing Co.

Ravindran, N., & Myers, B.J. (2012). Cultural influences on perceptions of health, illness, and disability: A review and focus on autism. *Journal of Child and Family Studies, 21*(2), 311–319. doi:10.1007/s10826-011-9477-9

Reichow, B., Halpern, J.I., Steinhoff, T.B., Letsinger, N., Naples, A., & Volkmar, F.R. (2012). Characteristics and quality of autism websites. *Journal of Autism and Developmental Disorders, 42*(6), 1263–1274. doi:10.1007/s10803-011-1342-6

Repacholi, B.M., Meltzoff, A.N., Rowe, H., & Toub, T.S. (2014). Infant, control thyself: Infants' integration of multiple social cues to regulate their imitative behavior. *Cognitive Development, 32*, 46–57. doi:10.1016/j.cogdev.2014.04.004

Robins, D.L., Fein, D., & Barton, M.L. (2009). *The Modified Checklist for Autism in Toddlers, Revised, with Follow-up.* Retrieved from http://www.autismspeaks.org/sites/default/files/docs/sciencedocs/m-chat/m-chat-r_f.pdf?v=1

Robins, D.L., Fein, D., Barton, M.L., & Green, J.A. (2001). The Modified Checklist for Autism in Toddlers: An initial study investigating the early detection of autism and pervasive developmental disorders. *Journal of Autism and Developmental Disorders, 31*(2), 131–144. doi:10.1023/A:1010738829569

Rogers, S.J., & Dawson, G. (2010). *Early Start Denver Model for children with autism: Promoting language, learning, and engagement.* New York, NY: Guilford Press.

Rogers, S.J., & Vismara, L. (2014). Interventions for infants and toddlers at risk for autism spectrum disorder. In F.R. Volkmar, S.J. Rogers, R. Paul, & K.A. Pelphrey (Eds.), *Handbook of autism and pervasive developmental disorders: Assessment, interventions, and policy* (4th ed., Vol. 2, pp. 739–765). New York, NY: Wiley.

Rosetti, L. (2006). *The Rossetti Infant-Toddler Language Scale.* East Moline, IL: LinguiSystems.

Rothbart, M.K., & Bates, J.E. (2006). Temperament. In W. Damon, R. Lerner, & N. Eisenberg (Eds.), *Handbook of child psychology: Social, emotional, and personality development* (6th ed., Vol. 3, pp. 99–166). New York, NY: Wiley.

Rothbart, M.K., Posner, M.I., & Kleras, J. (2006). Temperament, attention, and the development of self-regulation. In K. McCartney & D. Phillips (Eds.), *Blackwell handbook of early childhood development.* Hoboken, NJ: Wiley-Blackwell.

Rush, D.D., & Shelden, M.L. (2011). *The early childhood coaching handbook.* Baltimore, MD: Paul H. Brookes Publishing Co.

Rutter, M., Le Couteur, A., & Lord, C. (2003). *Autism Diagnostic Interview–Revised.* Los Angeles, CA: Western Psychological Services.

Sacrey, L.R., Armstrong, V.L., Bryson, S.E., & Zwaigenbaum, L. (2014). Impairments to visual disengagement in autism spectrum disorder: A review of experimental studies from infancy to adulthood. *Neuroscience and Biobehavioral Reviews, 47,* 559–577. doi:10.1016/j.neubiorev.2014.10.011

Schaaf, R.C., & Lane, A.E. (2014). Toward a best-practice protocol for assessment of sensory features in ASD. *Journal of Autism and Developmental Disorders, 45*(5), 1380–1395. doi:10.1007/s10803-014-2299-z

Schertz, H.H. (2005). Promoting joint attention in toddlers with autism: A parent-mediated developmental model. (Doctoral dissertation, Indiana University, 2005). *Dissertation Abstracts International, 66,* 3982.

Schertz, H.H., & Odom, S.L. (2007). Promoting joint attention in toddlers with autism: A parent-mediated developmental model. *Journal of Autism and Developmental Disorders, 37*(8), 1562–1575. doi:http://dx.doi.org/10.1007/s10803-006-0290-z

Schertz, H.H., Odom, S.L., Baggett, K.M., & Sideris, J.H. (2013). Effects of joint attention mediated learning for toddlers with autism spectrum disorders: An initial randomized controlled study. *Early Childhood Research Quarterly, 28*(2), 249–258. doi:10.1016/j.ecresq.2012.06.006

Schmitt, L., Heiss, C.J., & Campbell, E.E. (2008). A comparison of nutrient intake and eating behaviors of boys with and without autism. *Topics in Clinical Nutrition, 23*(1), 23–31. doi:10.1097/01.TIN.0000312077.45953.6c

Schreck, K.A., Williams, K., & Smith, A.F. (2004). A comparison of eating behaviors between children with and without autism. *Journal of Autism and Developmental Disorders, 34*(4), 433–438. doi:10.1023/B:JADD.0000037419.78531.86

Schreibman, L., & Ingersoll, B. (2011). Naturalistic approaches to early behavioral intervention. In D.G. Amaral, G. Dawson, & D.H. Geschwind (Eds.), *Autism spectrum disorders* (pp. 1056–1067). New York, NY: Oxford University Press.

Senju, A., & Csibra, G. (2008). Gaze following in human infants depends on communicative signals. *Current Biology, 18*(9), 668–671. doi:10.1016/j.cub.2008.03.059

Shetreat-Klein, M., Shinnar, S., & Rapin, I. (2014). Abnormalities of joint mobility and gait in children with autism spectrum disorders. *Brain and Development, 36*(2), 91–96. doi:10.1016/j.braindev.2012.02.005

Shic, F., Bradshaw, J., Klin, A., Scassellati, B., & Chawarska, K. (2011). Limited activity monitoring in toddlers with autism spectrum disorder. *Brain Research, 1380*, 246–254. doi:10.1016/j.brainres.2010.11.074

Shonkoff, J.P., & Phillips, D.A. (Eds.). (2000). *From neurons to neighborhoods: The science of early childhood programs.* Washington, DC: National Academy.

Shriberg, L.D., Paul, R., Black, L.M., & van Santen, J.P. (2011). The hypothesis of apraxia of speech in children with autism spectrum disorder. *Journal of Autism and Developmental Disorders, 41*(4), 405–426. doi:10.1007/s10803-010-1117-5

Skinner, B.F. (1957). *Verbal behavior.* Englewood Cliffs, NJ: Prentice Hall.

Sparaci, L., Stefanini, S., D'Elia, L., Vicari, S., & Rizzolatti, G. (2014). What and why understanding in autism spectrum disorders and Williams syndrome: Similarities and differences. *Autism Research, 7*(4), 421–432. doi:10.1002/aur.1370

Sroufe, L.A. (2000). Early relationships and the development of children. *Infant Mental Health Journal, 21*(1–2), 67–74. Retrieved from http://www.cpsccares .org/system/files/Early%20Relationships%20and%20 the%20Development%20of%20Young%20Children .pdf

Strain, P.S., Schwartz, I.S., & Barton, E. (2011). Providing interventions for young children with ASD: What we still need to accomplish. *Journal of Early Intervention, 33*(4), 321–333. doi:10.1177/1053815111429970

Strauss, K., Vicari, S., Valeri, G., D'Elia, L., Arima, S., & Fava, L. (2012). Parent inclusion in early intensive behavioral intervention: The influence of parental stress, parent treatment fidelity and parent-mediated generalization of behavior targets on child outcomes. *Research in Developmental Disabilities, 33*(2), 688–703. doi:10.1016/j.ridd.2011.11.008

Sucksmith, E., Roth, I., & Hoekstra, R.A. (2011). Autistic traits below the clinical threshold: Re-examining the broader autism phenotype in the 21st century. *Neuropsychology Review, 21*(4), 360–389. doi:10.1007/ s11065-011-9183-9

Sundberg, M.L. (2008). *VB-MAPP verbal behavior milestones assessment and placement program: A language and social skills assessment program for children with autism or other developmental disabilities.* Concord, CA: AVB.

Thompson, R.A., & Meyer, S. (2014). Socialization of emotion and emotion regulation in the family. In J.J. Gross (Ed.), *Handbook of emotion regulation* (pp. 173–186). New York, NY: Guilford Press.

Tomlin, A., Koch, S.M., Raches, C., Minshawi, N.F., & Swiezy, N.B. (2013). Autism screening practices among early intervention providers in Indiana. *Infants & Young Children, 26*(1), 74–88. doi:10.1097/ IYC.0b013e31827842b1

Trillingsgaard, A., Sørensen, E.U., Němec, G., & Jørgensen, M. (2005). What distinguishes autism spectrum disorders from other developmental disorders before the age of four years? *European Child and Adolescent Psychiatry, 14*(2), 65–72. doi:10.1007/ s00787-005-0433-3

Tronick, E. (2013). Typical and atypical development: Peek-a-boo and blind selection. In K. Brandt, B.D. Perry, S. Seligman, & E. Tronick (Eds.), *Infant and early childhood mental health: Core concepts and clinical practice* (pp. 55–69). Arlington, VA: American Psychiatric Publishing.

Tsao, L., Davenport, R., & Schmiege, C. (2012). Supporting siblings of children with autism spectrum disorders. *Early Childhood Education Journal, 40*(1), 47–54. doi:10.1007/s10643-011-0488-3

University of Utah College of Education. (2015). *Terrell Howard Bell.* Retrieved from http://education.utah. edu/alumni/profiles/terrell-bell.php

Vallotton, C., & Ayoub, C. (2011). Use your words: The role of language in the development of toddlers' self-regulation. *Early Childhood Research Quarterly, 26*(2), 169–181. doi:10.1016/j.ecresq.2010.09.002

Vanvuchelen, M., Van Schuerbeeck, L., Roeyers, H., & De Weerdt, W. (2013). Understanding the mechanisms behind deficits in imitation: Do individuals with autism know "what" to imitate and do they know "how" to imitate? *Research in Developmental Disabilities, 34*(1), 538–545. doi:10.1016/j.ridd.2012.09.016

Vivanti, G., & Hamilton, A. (2014). Imitation in autism spectrum disorders. In F.R. Volkmar, R. Paul, A. Klin, & D. Cohen (Eds.), *Handbook of autism and pervasive developmental disorders: Assessment, interventions, and policy* (4th ed., Vol. 2, pp. 278–301). Hoboken, NJ: Wiley.

Vivanti, G., Trembath, D., & Dissanayake, C. (2014). Mechanisms of imitation impairment in autism spectrum disorder. *Journal of Abnormal Child Psychology, 42*(8), 1395–1405. doi:10.1007/s10802-014-9874-9

Wagner, A.L., Wallace, K.S., & Rogers, S.J. (2014). Developmental approaches to treatment of young children with autism spectrum disorder. In J. Tarbox, D.R. Dixon, P. Sturmey, & J.L. Matson (Eds.), *Handbook of early intervention for autism spectrum disorders: Research, policy, and practice* (pp. 501–542). New York, NY: Springer.

Wang, J., & Barrett, K.C. (2012). Mastery motivation and self-regulation during early childhood. In K.C. Barrett, N.A. Fox, & G. Morgan (Eds.), *Handbook of self-regulatory processes in development: New directions and international perspectives* (pp. 337–380). New York, NY: Psychology Press.

Watson, L.R., Crais, E.R., Baranek, G.T., Dykstra, J.R., & Wilson, K.P. (2013). Communicative gesture use in infants with and without autism: A retrospective home video study. *American Journal of Speech-Language Pathology, 22*(1), 25–39. doi:10.1044/1058-0360(2012/11-0145)

Wetherby, A.M. (1991). Profiling pragmatic abilities in the emerging language of young children. In T.M. Gallagher (Ed.), *Pragmatics of language: Clinical practice issues* (pp. 249–281). San Diego, CA: Singular.

Wetherby, A.M., Watt, N., Morgan, L., & Shumway, S. (2007). Social communication profiles of children with autism spectrum disorders late in the second year of life. *Journal of Autism and Developmental Disorders, 37*(5), 960–975. doi:10.1007/s10803-006-0237-4

Wetherby, A.M., & Woods, J. (2006). Early social interaction project for children with autism spectrum disorders beginning in the second year of life: A preliminary study. *Topics in Early Childhood Special*

Education, 26(2), 67–82. doi:10.1177/0271121406026 0020201

Wetherby, A.M., & Woods, J. (2008). Developmental approaches to treatment. In K. Chawarska, A. Klin, & F.R. Volkmar (Eds.), *Autism spectrum disorders in infants and toddlers: Diagnosis, assessment, and treatment* (pp. 170–206). New York, NY: Guilford Press.

Wieder, S., & Greenspan, S.I. (2001). The DIR (Developmental, Individual-difference, Relationship-based) approach to assessment and intervention planning. *Zero to Three, 21*, 11–19.

Williams, K.E., Hendy, H., & Knecht, S. (2008). Parent feeding practices and child variables associated with childhood feeding problems. *Journal of Developmental and Physical Disabilities, 20*(3), 231–242. doi:10.1007/s10882-007-9091-3

Winsper, C., & Wolke, D. (2014). Infant and toddler crying, sleeping and feeding problems and trajectories of dysregulated behavior across childhood. *Journal of Abnormal Child Psychology, 42*(5), 831–843. doi:10.1007/s10802-013-9813-1

Wolff, J.J., Botteron, K.N., Dager, S.R., Elison, J.T., Estes, A.M., Gu, H., … Piven, J. (2014). Longitudinal patterns of repetitive behavior in toddlers with autism. *Journal of Child Psychology and Psychiatry, 55*(8), 945–953. doi:10.1111/jcpp.12207

Woods, J. (2008). Providing early intervention services in natural environments. *ASHA Leader, 13*(4), 14–17. Retrieved from http://www.cdd.unm.edu/ecspd/portal /docs/tta/ASHA%20Provide%20EI%20in%20 Natural%20Environ.pdf

Woods, J., Wilcox, M., Friedman, M., & Murch, T. (2011). Collaborative consultation in natural environments: Strategies to enhance family-centered supports and services. *Language, Speech, and Hearing Services in Schools, 42*(3), 379–392. doi:10.1044/0161-1461(2011/10-0016)

Yerys, B.E., Wallace, G.L., Harrison, B., Celano, M.J., Giedd, J.N., & Kenworthy, L.E. (2009). Set-shifting in children with autism spectrum disorders: Reversal shifting deficits on the Intradimensional /Extradimensional Shift Test correlate with repetitive behaviors. *Autism, 13*(5), 523–538. doi:10.1177 /1362361309335716

Young, G.S., Rogers, S.J., Hutman, T., Rozga, A., Sigman, M., & Ozonoff, S. (2011). Imitation from 12 to 24 months in autism and typical development: A longitudinal Rasch analysis. *Developmental Psychology, 47*(6), 1565–1578. doi:10.1037/a0025418

Zhou, Q., Chen, S.H., & Main, A. (2012). Commonalities and differences in the research on children's effortful control and executive function: A call for an integrated model of self-regulation. *Child Development Perspectives, 6*(2), 112–121. doi:10.1111/j.1750-8606.2011.00176.x

Zwaigenbaum, L., Bryson, S., Lord, C., Rogers, S., Carter, A., Carver, L., … Yirmiya, N. (2009). Clinical assessment and management of toddlers with suspected autism spectrum disorder: Insights from studies of high-risk infants. *Pediatrics, 123*(5), 1383–1391. doi:10.1542/peds.2008-1606

Zwaigenbaum, L., Bryson, S., Rogers, T., Roberts, W., Brian, J., & Szatmari, P. (2005). Behavioral manifestations of autism in the first year of life. *International Journal of Developmental Neuroscience, 23*(2), 143–152. doi:10.1016/j.ijdevneu.2004.05.001

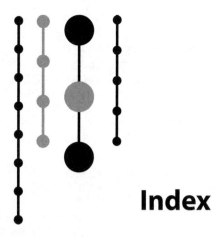

Index

Page numbers followed by *f* and *t* indicate figures and tables, respectively.

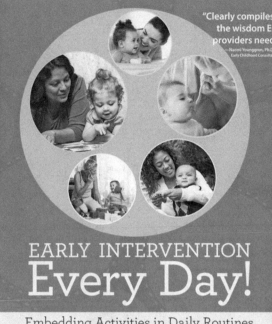